MW00753486

PERSONALITY
STYLE
AT WORK

PERSONALITY STYLE AT WORK

The Secret to Working with (Almost) Anyone

KATE WARD

NEW YORK   CHICAGO   SAN FRANCISCO

LISBON   LONDON   MADRID   MEXICO CITY   MILAN

NEW DELHI   SAN JUAN   SEOUL   SINGAPORE

SYDNEY   TORONTO

The **McGraw·Hill** Companies

Copyright ©2012 by HRDQ. All rights reserved. Manufactured in the United States of America. Except as permitted under the United States Copyright Act of 1976, no part of this publication may be reproduced or distributed in any form or by any means, or stored in a data base or retrieval system, without the prior written permission of the publisher.

1 2 3 4 5 6 7 8 9 0   DOC/DOC 1 8 7 6 5 4 3 2

ISBN 978-0-07-179160-1
MHID   0-07-179160-4

e-book ISBN 978-0-07-179161-8
e-book MHID   0-07-179161-2

Book design by Mauna Eichner and Lee Fukui

HRDQ® and the HRDQ logo are registered trademarks of Organization Design and Development, Inc.

McGraw-Hill books are available at special quantity discounts to use as premiums and sales promotions, or for use in corporate training programs. To contact a representative please e-mail us at bulksales@mcgraw-hill.com.

This book is printed on acid-free paper.

To my parents, Janet and Frank Lewis,
for their lifelong love and support

Contents

FOREWORD   ix

INTRODUCTION   xiii

PART I

UNDERSTANDING PERSONALITY STYLE

One   WHAT IS PERSONALITY STYLE AND
        WHY DOES IT MATTER?   3

Two   THE TWO DIMENSIONS OF PERSONALITY:
        ASSERTIVENESS AND EXPRESSIVENESS   17

PART II

HOW TO RECOGNIZE YOUR OWN AND OTHERS' PERSONALITY STYLE

Three RECOGNIZING PERSONALITY STYLES   35

Four   WHEN STYLES COLLIDE   57

PART III

PERSONALITY STYLE IN THE REAL WORLD— A STYLE FOR EVERY SITUATION

Five   STYLES AND COMMUNICATION   79

Six   MANAGING AND LEADING PEOPLE OF
         EVERY STRIPE AND COLOR   99

Seven WORKING ON TEAMS   125

Eight YOU CAN GET ALONG WITH YOUR BOSS   149

PART IV
USING PERSONALITY STYLES TO
ADVANCE YOUR CAREER

Nine PLANT WHERE YOU'LL BLOOM   177

Ten BLOOM WHERE YOU'RE PLANTED   201

WHAT'S YOUR PERSONALITY STYLE?   225

NOTES   229

ACKNOWLEDGMENTS   233

INDEX   235

FOREWORD

Most of my working career has been spent studying how to deal effectively with different personalities. It is fascinating work, and even after 40 years of professional practice, I am sometimes surprised by the hunger for information on the topic.

The reason for this seemingly endless need to understand our interactions with our fellow human beings is one of those simple, yet profound, facts of life; because our success in "meshing" with others ultimately determines the success we will have in both our professional and personal lives.

After all, a basic understanding of the dynamics of personality styles is a key competency shared by the very best managers, the most successful salespeople, and the most productive and respected employees. Often, those who possess these skills use them in their personal lives to get the same positive results among family and friends.

But despite all the obvious benefits of taking time to really understand the dynamics of what unites, divides, satisfies, or angers different personality types and styles, most of us never really figure people out. For the most part, we just ricochet through life's relationships. We get along great with some people; we refuse to deal with others; or we try to deal with certain people as little as possible.

But what if you were offered a better way to deal with the differences between people? What if you were offered a simple, but proven, way to build rapport with everyone: a way to eliminate personality conflicts and to make business mutually beneficial instead of a contest of wills?

The book you're holding contains this information and much more. After reading *Personality Style at Work*, I assure you that you'll see people differently; you'll understand them better, and be able to deal with them in a way that will turn every interpersonal encounter into an opportunity for a mutual win.

Why can I promise this?

Because your communication is only as good as your understanding of the person you're communicating with.

This book provides many easy-to-remember ways to understand and interact successfully with different personalities. While its focus is mainly on the workplace, you'll find that the book is also something of a people-watcher's field guide that you can use to better communicate with everyone you encounter, no matter the venue.

To illustrate my point, here are two examples from my files:

Case 1: A mortgage broker had a client who kept postponing and cancelling meetings at the last minute. When the two finally met, the broker quickly analyzed his client's personality style using a few simple techniques. He adapted to her personality style and quickly closed the deal. The client told her broker best friend: "When I made the appointments, I dreaded each time the date neared. But I actually had a wonderful time. You really made learning about the loan process interesting, and I trust you. You have a gift for communication." The broker ended up getting four referrals from the client, even before he finished her refinancing.

Case 2: I have an entrepreneur friend who is extremely outgoing and animated. He is fond of hearty, two-handed handshakes and calling people by their first names. He asks about spouses and kids even if he barely knows the person with whom he's having a conversation. My other friend is a terrific businessman, but he's more of a team-builder. He is warm but restrained, pleasant but not pushy, and he's more interested in genuine dialogue than slaps on the back. I put the two friends together to discuss a business deal. Can you guess how the meeting went? That's right. Both were uncomfortable, and of course, they didn't reach agreement for reasons that had nothing to do with the facts of the proposal.

My files are filled with real-life examples like the two above, examples that demonstrate the power and potential of the concepts presented in this book. You can absolutely use these personality concepts presented here to resolve differences, increase sales, maximize strengths, and enjoy fuller, more successful lives.

Personality Style at Work is a book you will use to build a personality style bridge in any situation, whether you're asking for a raise, closing a sale, developing a big work project, interacting with family and friends, or providing service to customers.

An additional benefit of your new personality style expertise and your increased ability to help others feel more comfortable in their interactions with you is adaptability. Adaptability occurs when you step out of your own comfort zone—your own personality style preferences—to meet another's needs.

Some of us adapt easily and naturally; others must work at it because lifelong habits of competition and conflict are not altered overnight. But it's doable *if* you're committed to learning and using these valuable techniques.

And here's a surprise benefit of the work that you put into understanding your personality style and the personality style of others. When you are adaptable and work to meet the needs of others, you are likely to find that *your* needs will be met as well! That's a benefit we can all live with!

> DR. TONY ALESSANDRA,
> author of *The Platinum Rule* and *The NEW Art of Managing People*

Introduction

Have you ever wondered why it is that you seem to get along with some people and not with others? Or why it is that you can inspire and motivate one person so easily, yet you just can't seem to get through to another? The answer lies in your personality style, a predictable set of behaviors that defines how others see you as you go about doing what you do. Your style—a preference for behaving one way rather than another—governs the way you lead others, participate in teamwork, communicate, make decisions, and manage change; it even governs the way you learn. Personality style influences the type of work you enjoy and the people you like to be around. But when people with diverse personality styles have to work together, well, that can be a recipe for real problems.

Maybe you get frustrated when things change too slowly, while the rest of your team thinks you move too fast. Or maybe you prefer detail, while your colleague is one of those big-picture idea types—all sizzle and no steak. Perhaps you prefer to take things in and consider all the options before making a decision, yet you work for a boss who's a mile-a-minute ball of energy and demands a quick response to everything. Or maybe social interaction is important to you—it's one of the reasons you enjoy your work, after all—and it irks you that you don't hear so much as a "good morning" from your coworkers at the start of each day.

Sound familiar? It should, because conflict, miscommunication, leadership failure, lack of engagement, high turnover, quality problems, and even poor individual and team performance can all have as their root cause a difference in personality "fit" between coworkers.

If you want to reach your full potential as a leader, manager, supervisor, or team player, you have to learn to work effectively with everyone. But there are some people whom you get along with more easily than others. The research into personality style gives clues as to why this is so. When you interact with people who share your style, you're on the same wavelength, so to speak, and you develop an almost instant rapport. But when you interact with people whose style is different from your own, that's when things can begin to unravel. Understanding your own style is the first step toward figuring out ways to work more effectively with others. And when you know others' styles, you can more easily adapt your behaviors in order to create more harmonious and fruitful working relationships.

Your personality style also influences the kinds of careers and environments (cultures) in which you are likely to thrive. When you use your strengths, you tend to feel more energized and satisfied with your work. But if you're not in an ideal environment, knowledge of personality styles will show you how you can adapt to the climate in order to minimize its negative effects on your job satisfaction.

What makes this book unique is the proven, research-based four-quadrant HRDQ Personality Style Model on which it is based. The model is featured in numerous workshop and self-assessment products published by HRDQ, which has administered these assessments to more than one million people. It is easy to use and understand, and it provides language that serves as a springboard for developing productive working relationships with others. However, its simplicity underlies its power to help people be better communicators, leaders, decision makers, motivators, and influencers and helps to explain why it is used for employee training by organizations of almost every type and size, both domestically and globally.

This book includes an assessment at the back that you can take to identify your style. You may be tempted to immediately jump to the end of the book and take the assessment; that in and of itself reveals something about your personality style! However, I recommend that you hold off, be patient, and read the entire book before taking the assessment in order to get a more balanced perspective on all the styles instead of being too focused on your own style.

Whether you read the book from beginning to end or jump around, picking and choosing the topics that interest you most, I hope you come away with the confidence to use your knowledge of personality styles to maximize your effectiveness in the workplace.

PART I

UNDERSTANDING

PERSONALITY

STYLE

One

WHAT IS
PERSONALITY STYLE
AND WHY DOES
IT MATTER?

P erhaps the best way to both illustrate and explain personality style (at least as humans experience it) is through a simple and probably familiar slice-of-life vignette.

You're riding an elevator down to the third floor in a standard office building. The elevator is carrying a full load of your colleagues, who are headed to their own meetings or out to lunch. Suddenly, the elevator stops between the fourth and fifth floors, and it won't budge. Someone, perhaps the office jokester, immediately rolls out a tension-breaking quip. "So, I guess you're all wondering why I called this meeting," the funny man says with a deadpan, business-as-usual tone. Everyone laughs as a few more captives offer jokes of their own; then the personality types of the individual riders begin to emerge.

One person reaches for the emergency phone to call for help. Someone else suggests a game to play while waiting to be rescued. Another person, partly in jest but with a worrying bit of real possibility, offers a rough estimate of how long it might take for people to use up all the oxygen in the elevator. A fourth person asks if everyone is OK and offers gum or perhaps water from an unopened bottle of water just purchased in the office lunchroom vending machine.

This scenario—getting stuck in an elevator with a bunch of strangers or colleagues—is so common that you may have an immediate connection to the story or even have a similar story of your own that you could relate. Perhaps you've even wondered about two key questions that the story illustrates:

1. Why do people react so differently to the same situation?

2. Why do people exhibit the same behaviors again and again, no matter what the situation?

Answering these questions is the purpose of this book, and the answer is found right in the title: personality styles. So what is personality? The precise answer to that question might fill a moderately large academic library. Here is the definition from the American Psychological Association:

> *Personality is the unique psychological quality of an individual that influences a variety of characteristic behavior patterns (both overt and covert) across different situations and over time.*[1]

In other words, personality is the *consistent* pattern of thoughts, feelings, and behaviors that makes a person unique. Personality isn't a reflection of intelligence, and it's not a measure of skills or abilities.

If you are a parent of more than one child, you can attest to the fact that each child is different. Often your children's personalities are apparent practically from the moment they are born. One child is happy and never fussy from the day she's born. Your second child seems to have been born with a mandate to try to sleep as little as possible and cry at every possible opportunity. Does any of this sound familiar?

Or, observe how your friends interact with others. Do some of your friends perpetually worry about something, while others seem to be unfailingly carefree and fun-loving? This is another example of how different personalities are apparent in everyday situations. While some scientists believe that personality is set from birth, others believe that outside influences shape your personality over time. This nature versus nurture debate is unlikely to be settled anytime soon. Whether you believe that personality is wired from birth or that life experiences fundamentally change your personality, this book will help you because its focus is on using *observable behaviors* to recognize your own and others' personality styles. Personality style is the way a person acts when he or she is able to do things his or her own way. Most people are consistent enough in their behavior to allow you to predict their behavior. With that knowledge, you can change your behavior in any given situation to minimize misunderstandings and improve communication.

KEY DEVELOPMENTS IN
UNDERSTANDING PERSONALITY

As noted, this is not the first book to consider the development of personality and how personality styles affect our lives and our relationships, and it's certainly not meant to serve as a reference tool or textbook. For that, I recommend *Personality: Classic Theories and Modern Research* by Howard S. Friedman and Miriam W. Schustack (Prentice Hall, 5th ed., 2010). Explorations of personality and the source of its development in humans can be traced at least back to the Greek physician Hippocrates more than 2,400 years ago.

Hippocrates (c. 460 BC–c. 377 BC) was a Greek physician who suggested that our personality was affected by the balance and flow of various bodily fluids (humors) through the body. Hippocrates also associated each personality temperament with one of the four elements (fire, air, water, and earth; see Figure 1.1).

Hippocrates believed that people with a higher concentration of *yellow bile* were *choleric*. These people tended to have more energy and to be more bold and ambitious than others. Those with more *blood* tended to be more *sanguine* and exhibited optimistic, impulsive, and pleasure-seeking characteristics. *Phlegmatic* people were thought to have an abundance of *phlegm* and could be spotted because they were calm, quiet, and kind. Anyone with high levels of *black bile*, Hippocrates labeled as *melancholic*, since people with this personality were usually independent, introspective, and more apt to be perfectionists (see Table 1.1).

While Hippocrates' science and labels were incorrect, he was right about the four basic temperaments found in human nature, and so this theory has endured for 2,400 years. In fact, it wasn't until 1926

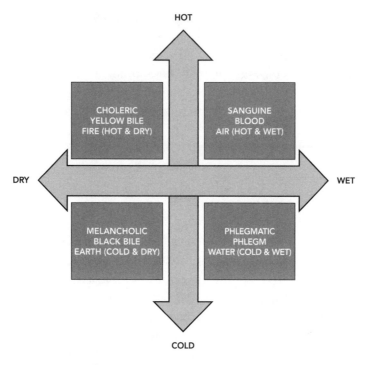

Figure 1.1 **Hippocrates' Four Humors**

that William Moulton Marston refined and described precisely the four humors that Hippocrates described.

Carl Jung (1875–1961) was a Swiss psychiatrist and philosopher whose work was influenced by Hippocrates' four humors. He was the first person to label and describe the concepts of introverted and extroverted personality types. These were paired with four functions—feeling, thinking, sensation, and intuition—to create

Table 1.1: **Characteristics of Each Humor**

Temperament	Humor	Element	Qualities (Dimensions)	Personality
Choleric	Yellow bile	Fire	Hot, dry	Volatile, ambitious
Sanguine	Blood	Air	Hot, wet	Cavalier, optimistic
Phlegmatic	Phlegm	Water	Cold, moist	Even-tempered, unhurried
Melancholic	Black bile	Earth	Cold, wet	Introspective, skeptical

William Moulton Marston lived from May 9, 1893 to May 2, 1947. In addition to his work as a psychologist, Marston was an inventor and a writer. He created the device that became the modern polygraph—the lie detector test. And for something completely different, he created the comic book character Wonder Woman.

eight personality types. Jung's work, in turn, influenced many others, including Katharine Cook Briggs and her daughter, Isabel Briggs Myers, who developed The Myers-Briggs Type Indicator (MBTI).

William Moulton Marston (1893–1947) published a book in 1928 called *Emotions of Normal People*. Prior to the publication of this book, most research into personality and behavior had been focused on the criminally insane. Marston thought that an understanding of personality was important for everyone, so he focused his attention on observable and measurable behavior that anyone might notice and interpret. Based on his research, he suggested that behavior should be categorized into four basic styles based on two separate personality dimensions.

He defined one dimension as the individual's perception of the environment around him—that is, whether it was favorable or unfavorable. The other dimension he defined was the individual's perception of his own power within the environment, or whether the person viewed himself as more powerful or less powerful within the environment.

Over time, these dimensions were further refined and different names or labels emerged. The research team at HRDQ called these dimensions assertiveness and expressiveness. The assertiveness dimension is the degree of effort you make to influence others, while the expressiveness dimension is the degree of effort you make when revealing your emotions to others. When put together, these elements form a quartet of personality dimensions, and it is these four quadrants of personality that are the basis of the HRDQ Personality Style Model used in this book:

- *Direct:* high assertiveness and low expressiveness
- *Spirited:* high assertiveness and high expressiveness

- *Considerate:* low assertiveness and high expressiveness
- *Systematic:* low assertiveness and low expressiveness

HRDQ Personality Style Model

The HRDQ Personality Style Model (see Figure 1.2) is built upon a long history of personality investigation, research, and theory, and it has been tested and applied in corporate and business settings around the world for many years.

The model assumes that individuals have specific, established, stable personalities that drive their behaviors. In other words, given a choice about how to behave in a given situation, an individual's personality style guides her behavior. While the model focuses on describing how the different personality styles behave in a work setting, the concepts are easily transferable to other settings, including

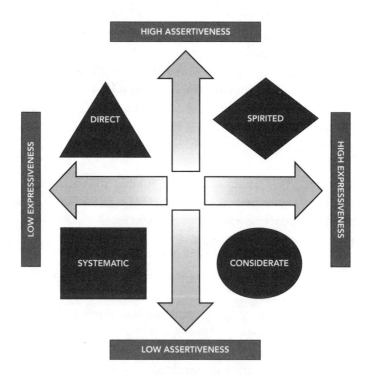

Figure 1.2 The HRDQ Personality Style Model

interactions with family and friends. Chapter 2 provides a complete explanation of the two dimensions of expressiveness and assertiveness and the four personality styles that are formed when you combine them.

DOES PERSONALITY STYLE MATTER?

Yes, personality style does matter! Whether you admit it or not, we are constantly sizing other people up, assessing what we like and dislike about other people, and categorizing people as those we get along with and those we don't. Most of the time, this sizing-up process is unconscious, but making it a conscious process can be helpful, especially in a workplace situation.

For example, understanding the source of the tension between you and your boss and making appropriate changes in your behavior might improve the situation and make it easier to show up for work every day. You never know, it might even save your job!

By understanding the personality styles, you'll be able to make conscious choices about your behavior and increase the likelihood that you will achieve your goals. You will also be able to establish realistic expectations about how to interact with a boss, coworker, team member, or even family member and minimize the possibility of misunderstandings.

Here's how using personality style works in the real world. Let's say a coworker of yours makes decisions in a slow and methodical way that you find annoying. Instead of creating a conflict with the coworker, your understanding of personality styles leads you to add extra time for decision making whenever possible. Your solution is based on a conscious decision about your coworker's style and your knowledge that asking this coworker to make a quick decision causes unproductive stress.

Or, if you know that a coworker prefers to dive right into work in the morning, while you prefer to chat and catch up on the news before "easing into" your day, you simply adjust your interactions with this coworker to fit his style. Thus, instead of a morning chat, you might schedule a more agreeable time to interact with this coworker.

THE DANGER OF STEREOTYPING

While understanding and applying personality styles can be extremely valuable, you should always remember to use the personality style model as a tool, not a rule. Nothing bugs people more than to be pigeonholed into a single behavior pattern or treated as if their personality interchangeable with that of anyone else with a similar personality style. While most of us have one dominant style, the reality is that we all have a little bit of each of the four styles within us. That's why it is shortsighted to stereotype. Every person wants to be treated as a unique individual, so don't use personality styles to

- Tell people what they're thinking or feeling.
- Decide for others how they should think, feel, or behave in a particular situation.
- Analyze others' motivations and behaviors with them.
- Encourage others to be more like you.

You should use the personality style model to guide your own behavior, not to try to mold or change other people's behaviors.

BENEFITS OF UNDERSTANDING AND APPLYING PERSONALITY STYLE

It's easy to see why recognizing different personality styles and adjusting your approach might have many benefits. For example, you can adjust or flex your behavior so that you relate to others in ways that they understand and appreciate. You can communicate effectively with people with each style in ways that build rapport and minimize conflict. You can determine the best person for a particular task by taking advantage of people's natural preferences and strengths, and avoid assigning tasks that would emphasize their shortcomings. And you can increase your self-awareness to identify and build on your unique strengths and in the process feel more energized and satisfied in your work.

Understanding and applying the personality style model is like being a chameleon—you can change color (adjust your behavior) to fit into your immediate surroundings, but your basic shape (personality style) always remains the same. Here are some examples.

1. Personality Styles in a Conflict

Molly and Elliot are two physicians' assistants who work in a busy dermatologist's office. They both see many patients a day, and they both are very competent in their work. They respect each other's skills, but they tend to clash frequently about the way they interact with patients. Elliot feels that many patients are nervous and appreciate a warm and personal demeanor. As a result, Elliot's patients often share intimate details about their lives with him. Molly thinks Elliot's demeanor is intrusive and unprofessional; she takes a clinical approach because she believes that patients are more comfortable with a medical professional who is calm and cool. They both believe they are right, and they believe that the office should present a consistent atmosphere, since patients can see either Molly or Elliot. The situation is at its worst when a patient's situation requires both Molly and Elliot to be present.

Molly and Elliot should address their conflict using a process that respects both individuals' points of view and doesn't devalue other personality styles. They should engage in a discussion aimed at finding a solution that meets their common interest, which in this case is meeting the needs of their patients. Once they recognize that they have the same goal, they will realize that the "right" style is the one that makes the patient feel most comfortable, and that the "right" style will vary from patient to patient. To be successful, Molly and Elliot must both be able to flex from their natural style occasionally in order to meet their patients' style preferences.

2. Trying to Persuade Others

Brooke and Jim are purchasing agents for a large manufacturer. Brooke wants to change the way potential suppliers are evaluated. This will be a big deal, since the process hasn't been changed in years. Brooke is a "take the bull by the horns" kind of person, and once she decides that something should happen, it usually does. Jim doesn't usually have strong opinions, but in this case he is adamant that the process works well as it is and refuses to consider any change. He digs in his heels as Brooke challenges him.

Brooke: "Why are you being so stubborn about this?"
Jim: "Why are you trying to fix something that isn't broken? We have enough work to do as it is."
Brooke: "But this will ultimately increase and improve our efficiency."
Jim: "I don't know what your problem is. I'm already efficient."

If Brooke had been familiar with personality styles and how to use them, she would have recognized that Jim's style preference means that he is more comfortable going slowly and analyzing something in depth before making a change. She might have enlisted Jim's support by asking him to evaluate the current process and then ask if he had any recommendations for improving it. By involving him up front rather than setting up a situation that looked like a snap decision to Jim, Brooke would have been more successful in persuading Jim to implement the proposed change.

3. Working on a Team

A team of geologists works for an international mining company. The team is loosely connected; team members are located in different countries and see each other in person only once a year. In between, they have weekly conference calls and occasional video meetings, but for the most part, they communicate by e-mail. It seems that they spend much of their time criticizing one another, quibbling with one another, or e-mailing behind one another's back about real or perceived slights. They have a hard time pulling together, yet they need the group to be more unified in order to use their collective influence to increase their visibility and reputation throughout the organization, as well as increase their budget for fieldwork.

If the team members applied their knowledge of personality styles, and in particular how the four personality styles have different ways of demonstrating trust to their team, team cohesiveness would be greater. In addition, by watching out for the typical negative patterns that each personality style is tempted to fall into—when under stress, for example—they would be able to avoid aggravating the situation. The team might also assign team roles to team members that draw on the strengths of their personality style and improve the overall team function and performance.

4. Working with Your Boss

Anita and Sam work in the public works department of a municipal office. Anita is the assistant director of the department, and Sam is in charge of the Recycling and Household Hazardous Waste Drop-Off Center. Sam loves his job and has many ideas about how to enhance the recycling services that the city offers to its residents. Sam knows that Anita is busy, so he tries to share all his ideas in one meeting to make the most of his time with her. Anita tells Sam that she doesn't have time to discuss his "pie in the sky" ideas. She isn't intentionally discouraging him, but she just can't deal with one more thing, especially one that's "nice to do" rather than "need to do" at the moment.

If Sam had recognized Anita's personality style and altered his style to meet hers, he could have been much more successful in working with her and getting his ideas considered. Since Anita's personality style prefers to focus on one thing at a time, Sam is sabotaging his efforts by sharing all his ideas at once.

5. Choosing Your Workplace

Donovan is a technical writer for a worldwide shipping company. He's been working steadily since college. He was a business major in school; his favorite semester was when he studied overseas. After graduation, he was hired by his current company and gradually worked his way into his current position. While Donovan appreciates having a job, he feels bored and restless. His work is starting to feel repetitive, and he is getting more and more frustrated by all the policies and procedures that are in place. He has lots of ideas for improvements that he believes would benefit the organization, but the organization's culture resists change, and that atmosphere is wearing him down.

If Donovan understood his personality style, he might seek additional responsibilities that would better match that personality style—ones that take advantage of his natural strengths and avoid tasks that he finds unappealing. In his case, he might pursue creating a blog or office newsletter to give him the variety and challenge he's looking for. And if and when he decides to consider another position, he should take into account how his personality style and the personality style of the prospective organization either suit each other or create the potential for a mismatch.

These examples show how you can apply the personality style model by flexing your behavior to improve your relationships with others at work and increase your satisfaction and performance on the job.

▶ POINTS TO REMEMBER

- ▶ Personality is the consistent pattern of thoughts, feelings, and behaviors that make a person unique. It's not a reflection of intelligence or a measure of skills or abilities.

- ▶ Personality style theory has been in existence for more than 2,400 years, beginning with Hippocrates in 400 B.C.

- ▶ The HRDQ Personality Style Model is based on the work of William Moulton Marston.

- ▶ There are four basic personality styles.

  - • *Direct:* high assertiveness and low expressiveness

  - • *Spirited:* high assertiveness and high expressiveness

  - • *Considerate:* low assertiveness and high expressiveness

14

- *Systematic:* low assertiveness and low expressiveness

▶ Use the personality style model as a tool, not a rule.

- Everybody has a little bit of each style in him, so although there are four basic styles, every person is unique.

- Use the model to guide your own behavior, not to force others to change.

▶ Ways to apply personality style information:

- Minimize conflicts and misunderstandings.

- Increase your ability to communicate effectively and persuade others.

- Work more productively in your team.

- Work more effectively with your boss.

- Choose a career that suits your personality style.

Two

THE TWO DIMENSIONS OF PERSONALITY: ASSERTIVENESS AND EXPRESSIVENESS

A s you learned in the previous chapter, the two dimensions that form the basis of personality style are assertiveness and expressiveness. Below is a scenario that presents both dimensions.

> Pam and Bruce work side by side in a call center. When asked to describe Pam, Bruce says, "She's a great worker. She really gets things done. She speaks her mind, so you always know exactly where you stand with her. But she can be kind of bossy; she's always telling me—well, telling everyone—what to do." When asked to describe Bruce, Pam says, "Bruce is such a likable guy. You can tell he really cares about his coworkers. I've only known him for a couple of weeks, but I feel like I've known him forever. In fact, I feel like I know a little bit too much about him, if you know what I mean."

In this example, Bruce described Pam as highly assertive, while Pam described Bruce as highly expressive. Think of each dimension as a continuum between two extremes. Most people will fall somewhere in between the two end points.

In practice, this means that some people are more expressive—they display their emotions more easily—while others are less expressive—they are more in control of their emotions. On the assertiveness side, people can be more or less assertive—some are more apt to *tell*, while others are more apt to *ask*. These tendencies are not right or wrong or good or bad; they're just different.

This chapter offers a detailed discussion of both dimensions, assertiveness and expressiveness, as the basis for a substantive discussion of the four very different personality styles that emerge when these two dimensions are combined. You will see clearly why someone who is highly assertive and highly expressive will behave very differently from someone who is both unassertive and unexpressive.

THE ASSERTIVENESS DIMENSION

The assertiveness dimension is a reflection of the effort you make to influence or control the thoughts and actions of others. What this means in practical terms is that if you rate yourself on the low end of the assertiveness dimension, it's likely that you don't focus on exerting influence over others. If, on the other hand, you rate yourself on the high end of the assertiveness dimension, then influence and control over others is probably a greater focus for you.

> Holly and Tasia are discussing space issues in their department. The department has added staff, and they are running out of room for workstations and storage.
>
> **Tasia:** "We're adding another employee next month. It's going to be really crowded."
> **Holly:** "The accounting department is right next to us, and it isn't growing at the same pace. We need to get some of that space."
> **Tasia:** "How can we do that? It's their space."
> **Holly:** "It's the company's space, not theirs. We're entitled to it as much as they are."
> **Tasia:** "I can't believe they would agree to that. Shouldn't we wait and see just how crowded it is once the new employee gets here?"
> **Holly:** "No way. I'm going to talk to their manager right now."

In general, if you are highly assertive, you are confident, ambitious, and action-oriented. If you are unassertive, you are more patient, easygoing, and deliberate in your thoughts and actions. Obviously, in this example, Holly is much more assertive than Tasia.

LOW-END ASSERTIVENESS BEHAVIORS

People who operate at the low end of the assertiveness continuum are receptive to others, but at the same time more cautious. They avoid taking risks, and they have little desire to influence others. Those who operate in this range dislike surprises or change and seek out predictable, stable situations.

While being less assertive has its place at work, the key is to avoid exhibiting extremely passive behavior. This behavior often arises from a need to be liked or excessive concern with what others think about you.

Typical passive body language includes a submissive stance with your head down and shoulders forward, slouching, a weak handshake, a nervous smile or laugh, a soft voice, and hesitations such as "um," "you know," "well," and the like. These are behaviors that you want to eliminate in the workplace.

Assertive or Aggressive—What's the Difference?

For some people, being assertive has a negative connotation, but being assertive is not the same thing as being aggressive. Someone who is assertive communicates with others in an honest and respectful way. Assertive people are comfortable expressing needs and persuading others without resorting to demeaning or disrespectful tactics.

Someone who is aggressive is more focused on getting what he wants and is not concerned about the feelings of others. An aggressive person might even resort to verbal attacks, shouting, or intimidation to make his point or get his way. Aggression is not part of the assertiveness continuum.

Assertive Language and Behaviors

Clearly, practicing assertive behavior in the workplace is desirable.[1] One way to do this is to make statements based on observable behavior rather than issuing opinions. For example, saying, "Yesterday, you arrived 20 minutes late, and you left 15 minutes early today" is better than saying, "You're lazy, and you don't care about your work."

Using language that is clear and concise is also a desirable outcome of an assertive approach in the workplace. For example, telling an employee, "Please prepare the report by 4:00 today," is far preferable to a vague instruction such as, "Don't you think you should prepare the report soon?"

THE EXPRESSIVENESS DIMENSION

In the scenario that follows, we have an example of both low expressive and high expressive behavior:

> Michael and Nathan are both web developers attending a networking event at the regional gathering of their professional association. Michael and Nathan introduce themselves to each other.
>
> **Michael:** "Hi, I'm Michael. Nice to meet you."
> **Nathan:** "Hi, Michael; I'm Nathan. Nice to meet you, too. I work at Studio 3. I've been there three years; it's a great place to work! How about you?"
> **Michael:** "I work at Central Bank."
> **Nathan:** "What did you think of the presentation? I thought it was fabulous! Well, except for that glitch with the projector. How embarrassing! Wouldn't you have felt awful?"
> **Michael:** "Probably not. I would have had a backup with me, and I'd have lined up an assistant to run the projector."
> **Nathan:** "Good thinking. I probably would have just panicked!"
> **Michael:** "I don't panic easily."

In this example, Michael displayed low expressiveness, while Nathan displayed highly expressive behavior. Those who interact with others at the low end of the expressiveness dimension control their emotions and feelings, preferring to restrain their emotions rather than share them openly with others. This restrained demeanor doesn't mean that these individuals don't feel the same emotions or can't have empathy; it's just that their natural tendency is to not disclose their feelings to others.

If you think you are at the low end of the expressiveness dimension, people may say you are more difficult to get to know than others who are more comfortable interacting at a higher level on the continuum.

If you think you fall at the high end of the expressiveness dimension, then you are probably someone who expresses emotions and feelings freely. In addition, most people would probably say that you are easy to get to know and that you present yourself as sociable, flexible, and demonstrative. Those at the high end of the expressiveness dimension are usually trusting and value close relationships.

People at the extreme low end or high end of the expressiveness dimension face challenges, just as those at both ends of the assertiveness dimension do. If you think you fall at the low end and self-disclosure is difficult for you, then you may have trouble developing rapport and getting to know other people.

If you think you fall at the extreme high end of the continuum, then you may have a tendency to blurt out every thought that comes into your head or say things that you'll regret later. You might also identify with a tendency to make decisions based solely on emotions, which is sometimes a problem in difficult or stressful situations.

FOUR DISTINCT STYLES FROM THE TWO DIMENSIONS

As noted at the beginning of this chapter and as shown in Figure 2.1, four very different personality styles emerge when the assertiveness and expressiveness dimensions are combined.

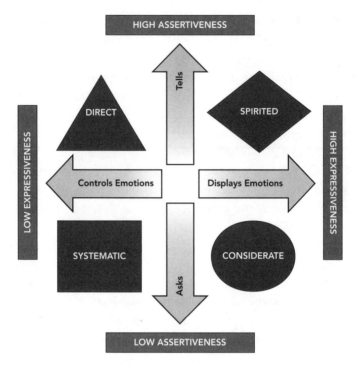

Figure 2.1 **Four Distinct Personality Styles**

Rather than starting with a discussion of the four styles (which does follow), the narrative examples given next offer a dramatic and more memorable introduction to these four styles:

- High assertiveness, low expressiveness: *Direct*
- High assertiveness, high expressiveness: *Spirited*
- Low assertiveness, high expressiveness: *Considerate*
- Low assertiveness, low expressiveness: *Systematic*

The frame for this narrative exploration of the four styles is a scenario in which a journalist is asked to write a "get to know your neighbor" feature story in the local newspaper. The journalist asks all four "neighbors" the same questions. The subjects of his interviews include

Virginia, a university professor

Stephen, a chef

Chloe, a bridal consultant

Ryan, an air traffic controller

Virginia, a University Professor

1. **What is your greatest accomplishment?**
   Virginia: I was the youngest person promoted to full professor at my school.

2. **What is your greatest failure?**
   Virginia: I tried to reorganize the department, and it wasn't approved by the dean.

3. **What do you like best about your job?**
   Virginia: I like that I'm basically my own boss—I don't have anyone looking over my shoulder the way I would if I worked in a corporate environment.

4. **What do you like least about your job?**
   Virginia: Grading papers.

5. **What is your favorite childhood memory?**
   Virginia: Beating my older brother when we were both in the debate club.

6. **How would you like to celebrate your next birthday?**
   Virginia: At a swanky restaurant with a group of friends.

7. **What is your ideal vacation?**
   Virginia: Staying at the Plaza Hotel in New York City, which I did last year.

8. **What is your favorite dog?**
   Virginia: German shepherd.

9. **What do you do for fun?**
   Virginia: I'm in a year-round competitive tennis league, and I'm trying to move up.

10. **What advice do you have for kids growing up today?**
    Virginia: Stay in school and get the best education you can.

Stephen, a Chef

1. **What is your greatest accomplishment?**
   Stephen: I hope I have even greater accomplishments ahead of me, but so far, I'd say my greatest accomplishment is opening my latest restaurant.

2. **What is your greatest failure?**
   Stephen: Ha, that's easy—closing my previous restaurant.

3. **What do you like best about your job?**
   Stephen: I love cooking; I really do. And when a restaurant critic has that "aha" moment—when she gets what I'm trying to do—that makes me feel really good. And a positive review doesn't hurt, either!

4. **What do you like least about your job?**
   Stephen: Managing the money—handling the accounting. Well, I don't actually—I hired someone else to do it, but I still have to be forced to pay attention to it.

5. **What is your favorite childhood memory?**
   Stephen: Going away to camp and doing all sorts of stuff for the first time—riding horses, sailing, archery, riflery, botany.

6. **How would you like to celebrate your next birthday?**
   Stephen: Las Vegas, baby!

7. **What is your ideal vacation?**
   Stephen: Taking a month in Europe with no plans and a Eurail Pass in my pocket, and then just seeing where the rails take me.

8. **What is your favorite dog?**
   Stephen: Saint Bernard.

9. **What do you do for fun?**
   Stephen: I love going to the theater, and going to movies is a close second.

10. **What advice do you have for kids growing up today?**
    Stephen: Do what you love.

Chloe, a Bridal Consultant

1. **What is your greatest accomplishment?**
   Chloe: At work? Or in life? My greatest accomplishment is raising two happy and healthy kids. But if you mean at work, then my greatest accomplishment was helping a bride plan her wedding at the same time as her mother died. It was so sad, but we did a lot to honor her mother.

2. **What is your greatest failure?**
   Chloe: I had a bride who bolted on the day of the wedding. It was a nightmare!

3. **What do you like best about your job?**
   Chloe: I love the satisfaction I get from helping brides plan one of the most important days of their lives.

4. **What do you like least about your job?**
   Chloe: When brides and their moms fight. Unfortunately, that happens more than I would like.

5. **What is your favorite childhood memory?**
   Chloe: Going to the cabin at the lake with my family every summer.

6. **How would you like to celebrate your next birthday?**
   Chloe: Potluck dinner with friends.

7. **What is your ideal vacation?**
   Chloe: I want to go to India to help the underprivileged. I've been saving up, and I should have enough money next year.

8. **What is your favorite dog?**
   Chloe: Anything from the shelter, preferably something white and fluffy that fits in my lap!

9. **What do you do for fun?**
   Chloe: I belong to a quilting group, and I go to exercise classes at the gym.

10. **What advice do you have for kids growing up today?**
    Chloe: Do something to help others; it will make you feel great.

Ryan, an Air Traffic Controller

1. What is your greatest accomplishment?
   Ryan: Every shift that is free from any abnormalities or incidents of any kind is an accomplishment.

2. What is your greatest failure?
   Ryan: I didn't get accepted into my first choice for college and had to settle for my second choice instead.

3. What do you like best about your job?
   Ryan: I like handling the complex problem of routing air traffic safely.

4. What do you like least about your job?
   Ryan: Obviously, when something goes wrong and there's an incident that we have to report.

5. What is your favorite childhood memory?
   Ryan: Winning the state spelling bee and going to Washington, D.C., to compete.

6. How would you like to celebrate your next birthday?
   Ryan: A home-cooked meal with my wife and a nice bottle of wine.

7. What is your ideal vacation?
   Ryan: Hiking to Machu Picchu.

8. What is your favorite dog?
   Ryan: A black Lab.

9. What do you do for fun?
   Ryan: I'm currently training for a marathon.

10. What advice do you have for kids growing up today?
    Ryan: Ignore peer pressure; set high goals and work to achieve them.

Each of these interviews paints a picture of a very different personality style. Virginia is a Direct, Stephen is a Spirited, Chloe is a Considerate, and Ryan is a Systematic.

With the stories as background, the rest of this chapter (and the book, really) explores the different characteristics of each style, including:

- The behaviors typically exhibited by people with each style

- What motivates (and demotivates) people with each style

- The communication and interaction characteristics of people with each style

- Most important, what you can do to work better with people with each style

Here's a brief description of each style.

Direct—High Assertiveness, Low Expressiveness

A Direct personality style is a combination of high assertiveness and low expressiveness. Those with a Direct style make a big effort to influence the thoughts and behaviors of others and control their emotions when relating to others. You might recognize someone with a Direct style by his competitive, decisive, and risk-taking nature. Those with a Direct style take the initiative and are motivated by power and authority. They also thrive on new challenges and resist routine or mundane tasks. Those with Direct personality styles may also avoid listening to the opinions of others. Virginia's Direct style is evident from her drive to achieve at a young age, her desire to be her own boss, her dislike of the routine work of grading papers, and her choice of status-oriented events for her birthday and her vacation.

Spirited—High Assertiveness, High Expressiveness

A Spirited personality style is a combination of high assertiveness and high expressiveness. Those with a Spirited style make a big effort to influence the thoughts and behaviors of others and display emotions when they relate to others. You might characterize someone with this style as enthusiastic, optimistic, talkative, impulsive, and emotional. In addition, someone with a Spirited personality is a great problem solver and very persuasive in motivating others. You might notice that those with a Spirited style thrive on the recognition, popularity, and praise that they receive from others. They also don't like structure or too many rules. In the case of Stephen, he exhibits his Spirited style by his love of creativity through cooking, his desire to receive positive reactions from customers and critics, his choosing an unplanned and unstructured vacation, and his advice, "Do what you love."

Considerate—Low Assertiveness, High Expressiveness

A Considerate personality style is a combination of low assertiveness and high expressiveness. Those with a Considerate style make little effort to influence the thoughts and behaviors of others, but do tend to display their emotions when relating to others. You might describe someone with this style as a loyal team worker who is also supportive of others, a great listener, friendly, reliable, and dependable. You may also notice that someone with a Considerate personality style tends to resist change and can be overly sensitive to criticism. Those with Considerate styles also dislike conflict and go to great lengths to maintain harmony, even sacrificing their own needs to achieve it. Chloe has a Considerate style, as evidenced by the satisfaction she gets from helping others, her dislike of conflict, her choice of a vacation to serve those in need, and her choice of nonwork activities that connect her with others.

Systematic—Low Assertiveness, Low Expressiveness

A Systematic personality style is a combination of low assertiveness and low expressiveness. Someone with a Systematic style makes little effort to influence the thoughts and behaviors of others and controls his emotions when relating to others. A description of a Systematic style might include the words *conscientious, careful, analytical,* and *accurate.* You may notice that someone with a Systematic personality style is excellent at implementation and follow-through (as long as a clear goal is articulated) and doesn't require much social interaction. Those with Systematic styles tend to avoid arguing and may give in to avoid conflict. Still, they are motivated by achieving the highest standards of performance. Ryan demonstrated his Systematic style through the satisfaction he gets from solving technical problems, his achieving high standards by winning the state spelling bee, his choosing a challenging activity for vacation and for fun, and his choice of a small, quiet dinner to celebrate his birthday.

Overusing Each Quadrant

Overusing either of the two dimensions discussed at the beginning of this chapter—expressiveness and assertiveness—often leads to ineffective behaviors. Overusing each of the four personality styles just discussed can also lead to counterproductive behaviors.

The four vignettes that follow illustrate what happens when each of the four personality styles is overdeveloped and overused. You will probably recognize the people and perhaps the situations described in each story.

The Overdeveloped Direct Style

Meet Dirk. He's the shift supervisor at an energy company. He's hot-tempered, demanding, and impatient. He's ambitious and thinks nothing of running over others to get what he wants. He's a know-it-all who is domineering and gets his own way by wearing others down. He disregards others' opinions and input and makes rash decisions based solely on his own interests. He makes little effort at self-control and restraint. He distrusts others and is loyal to no one. When he's at his worst, his coworkers describe him as a bully.

The Overdeveloped Spirited Style

Meet Felicity. She's a graphic designer. If she makes a deadline, it's by the skin of her teeth. She drives her coworkers nuts with her disorganization and lack of focus. She can't seem to keep her attention on one area for more than a few moments, and then she'll be distracted by a random thought or idea. The thing is, some of those random ideas are brilliant. However, most of them aren't, and she wastes a lot of time chasing after impractical ideas, dragging others along with her. She's always changing her mind about what her projects should look like. On top of that, she talks way too much—sometimes she shocks others with her lack of discretion. When she's at her worst, coworkers describe her as irresponsible, impulsive, and irrational.

The Overdeveloped Considerate Style

Meet Emily. She manages the help desk at a large research facility. Everyone likes Emily, but people walk all over her. She can't say no to a request, even if it's not really her responsibility. People know she is willing to help out, even if her own work suffers. She gets indecisive when she's stressed, which is often. She has an unrealistic idea of how long things will take, and she ends up feeling overwhelmed. Meanwhile, projects that she hasn't completed become urgent, stressing her out even more. She avoids conflict and gives in rather than face a confrontation. As a result, she bottles up her feelings. Her manager has suggested several ways to improve her work process, but she hates change, even if it would ultimately benefit her. At first, some of her coworkers urged her to stand up for herself when people made unreasonable requests, but now they've given up and just accept that she's destined to be a martyr.

The Overdeveloped Systematic Style

Meet Ethan. He's a computer programmer for an accounting software company. He is a stickler for following rules and procedures. He will never go outside the established system, and he won't let you do so either if he can help it. He doesn't appear to care about what other people think or feel; he prefers to operate alone because he believes that no one else can do as good a job as he can. He is critical of other people's work; he doesn't hesitate to let them know when their work contains a mistake, even on the smallest thing. When there's a problem, he gets overly focused on the details—he can't see the forest for the trees. As a result, he might be able to correct a symptom, but not the larger problem or issue. When he is stressed, he withdraws and gets even more firmly entrenched in his ways. When he's at his worst, his coworkers describe him as uptight, rigid, and stubborn.

CONCLUSION

As you can clearly see, individuals who overuse any of the four personality styles present real challenges in organizations. It's likely that you know workers, team members, or managers who exhibit these overdeveloped behaviors—perhaps some of these descriptions are even a little too close to home. Luckily, most of us are better rounded than these examples of individuals operating at the edges of the assertiveness and expressiveness dimensions. In fact, most people carry around just a little bit of each style within them. Once you recognize the common personality style links between each of us, you will find that it's easier to relate to most people on some level.

Note: There are many question-and-answer exercises in this book that are designed to help you apply the information to your own situation. Record your answers in a notebook (paper or electronic) for later reference and use. Here is the first activity.

EXERCISE: COMPARING YOURSELF TO OTHERS ON THE TWO DIMENSIONS

Think about a person you work with. Where would you place him or her on the assertiveness and expressive dimensions? Where would you place yourself on each dimension? Place a mark on each continuum in Figure 2.2 to indicate the relative assertiveness and expressiveness of you and the other person.

You can use this comparison for any number of people. The difference between the two marks on each continuum reflects the degree to which you may need to adjust your style to match the style of the other person.

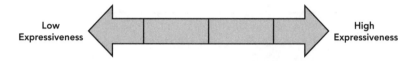

Figure 2.2 Comparing Yourself and Others on the
Assertiveness and Expressiveness Dimensions

▶ POINTS TO REMEMBER

▶ There are two dimensions to personality style: assertiveness and expressiveness.

▶ Assertiveness is the effort you make to influence or control the thoughts and actions of others.

▶ Expressiveness is the degree to which you control or express your emotions when relating to others.

▶ The combination of the two dimensions forms the four quadrants or four personality styles.

- High assertiveness and low expressiveness: *Direct*

- High assertiveness and high expressiveness: *Spirited*

- Low assertiveness and high expressiveness: *Considerate*

- Low assertiveness and low expressiveness: *Systematic*

PART II

HOW TO RECOGNIZE YOUR OWN AND OTHERS' PERSONALITY STYLE

Three

RECOGNIZING PERSONALITY STYLES

Sometimes someone's personality style is easy to recognize. Think of these four people, all of whom are on Gallup's list of people that Americans most widely admired in the twentieth century[1]: Margaret Thatcher, Martin Luther King, Jr., Mother Teresa, and Albert Einstein. Margaret Thatcher's nickname, the Iron Lady, suggests her Direct style. Martin Luther King's "I Have a Dream" speech epitomizes the Spirited outlook. Mother Teresa's compassion reveals her Considerate style, and Albert Einstein's tenacious problem-solving ability is a sign of his Systematic style. These familiar figures have defining characteristics that make their personality styles easy to identify.

But simply recognizing the personality styles of famous people is rather meaningless—what counts is identifying the styles of the people you interact with every day. And to actually benefit from applying the information, you need to recognize an individual's personality style accurately. That's why it's important to examine a wide range of signs, indicators, and clues. Here's an example:

Allison works for Justin. She learned about personality styles and guessed that Justin was a Systematic, based on the fact that he seemed to be like her—independent and not very emotional. So she prepared a detailed analysis of a recent single-market product launch. She collected extensive data and spent many hours organizing and evaluating the results. To her, it was obvious that the product launch was a failure. When she presented her conclusion to Justin, he glanced at it and said, "I've already decided that we're going to launch the product in all of our markets." Allison was stunned. "Don't you need to review the data? I think you might reach a different conclusion," she said. Justin replied, "Nope. I know what we need to do to make this profitable, and that's what we're going to do."

Allison's misreading of Justin's personality style hampered her effort to help him make a rational, logical decision about the product launch. When she was decoding his personality style, she saw only what she wanted to see, and, as a result, she made a miscalculation that negatively affected the outcome of the decision, in her opinion.

There are several ways to recognize another person's personality style. The first is to observe—look at his workspace, his body language, even how he learns. The second is to listen—you will hear clues in both his language and his tone of voice. The last way to determine another person's personality style, and perhaps the most revealing, is to interact with him—you will see clues in how this person participates (or not) as a team member, how he manages or supervises others (if he has that role), and how he manages his time. You may have a question at this point—what if I can't observe or interact with people face to face? For example, you may work from home, or you may work with colleagues who are located in another geographic region. You may interact with others primarily through phone and e-mail. At the end of this chapter, you'll find some tips for recognizing personality styles in a virtual or remote world where there is little or no face-to-face contact.

Observe Personality Style Clues

You may be able to identify other people's personality styles simply by observing them and their environments.

Workspace

First, take the "desk test"—try it out on yourself first, and then apply it to other people. Take a look at your own workspace. Read the

WAYS TO LEARN AT WORK

On-the-job

Job rotation or cross-training

Coaching and mentoring

Shadowing or observation

Problem-solving or brainstorming groups

Simulation activities

Workshops and classroom training

Conferences and seminars

E-learning

Independent research

User groups

Formal continuing education classes

following descriptions and choose the one that most closely reflects your workspace.

1. Your desk is messy! Papers are strewn everywhere, along with magazines, receipts, forms, books, and other things. The walls are covered with a variety of posters, inspirational sayings, notes and reminders, and so on. If you have space, there is a seating area where two people can sit next to each other.

2. Your desk is covered with paperwork, but it's organized in piles. On the wall, a large planning calendar hangs alongside your diplomas and awards. Family or personal photos are located discreetly in the corner. Your chair is substantial, and guest/visitor seating is located across from the desk.

3. Your desk is cluttered, but you know where everything is. Family photos are prominently displayed on your desk, along with mementos from events that are important to you. The walls are covered with serene landscapes, group photos, and other personal items. If there is a seating area, you have a comfy couch where you can talk with others side by side.

4. Your desk is tidy and clear of papers, except what you're currently working on. You clean off your desk every night, and your work files are extremely organized. Job-related information—charts, graphs, calendars, and other such material—is neatly displayed on the walls. You like to use the latest technology to work more efficiently whenever possible.

The first choice describes a Spirited work area, the second describes a Direct, the third describes a Considerate style, and the fourth choice describes a Systematic style. Examining someone's workspace provides a quick clue to her personality style.

How People Learn

Another way to determine an individual's personality style is to observe how he likes to learn. There are four basic learning styles: whether the person prefers to learn by doing or learn by thinking, and whether he prefers to learn in a group or on his own (see Figure 3.1).[2]

Direct Style Learning. People with the Direct style prefer to learn independently and by doing, rather than by thinking and reflecting. They want to take charge of their own learning, and they don't want

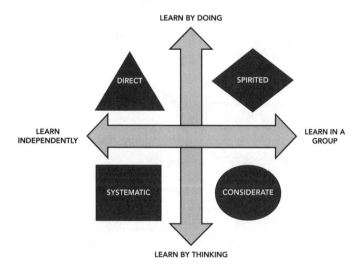

Figure 3.1 **How People Learn**

to waste time. So, if you notice that a coworker seems extremely bored or impatient in a training class, that is a clue that the person may have a Direct style. And if that person seems to learn by trial and error, that's another sign of a Direct style.

Spirited Style Learning. People with the Spirited style prefer to learn by doing, but with others. They are likely to enjoy being mentored, and they love attending conferences and workshops with people from outside the organization. If you notice someone who resists completing an online self-study program, that is a clue that the individual has a Spirited style.

Considerate Style Learning. People with the Considerate style prefer to learn by thinking and reflecting, but in a group. Considerate individuals usually enjoy traditional classroom training and team-building activities, as opposed to self-study programs or just jumping in and taking on a new project. If you are a manager and one of your employees requires a lot of hand-holding when you assign her a new project, that is a clue that the employee may have a Considerate style.

Systematic Style Learning. People with the Systematic style prefer to learn by independent thinking. Because of that, if you notice someone in a classroom training setting who is reluctant to participate, that person may have a Systematic style. These people generally prefer self-study options and often seek out web-based training or similar opportunities. They learn better with a structured approach than with an informal approach.

Body Language

Observing people's body language provides huge clues to their personality style. See if you can identify each person's personality style using the following scenario:

You have just been hired, and your new boss is introducing you to the other members of your team.

- Clark gives you a short handshake, briefly makes eye contact, says "Hello," and waits for you to respond.

- Christopher gives you a gentle handshake, makes eye contact briefly, then stands close to you and says, "Hi, how are you?"

- Melissa looks you directly in the eye, gives you a firm handshake, says "Nice to meet you," and then turns away.

- Tracy gives you a warm handshake and makes frequent eye contact. She stands close to you and says, "Hello; we're so glad to have you join us as part of our team."

Direct Style Body Language. People with a Direct style generally will make sustained eye contact with you. They have a firm handshake, and they tend to use strong and pronounced gestures to emphasize their points. They move quickly and maintain a larger personal space—the distance between you and them. In the example, Melissa displayed a Direct style.

Spirited Style Body Language. People with a Spirited style generally will make frequent eye contact with you. They have an enthusiastic handshake, and they use lots of gestures ("talk with their hands") when talking. They move quickly and maintain a close personal space—the distance between you and them. In the example, Tracy demonstrated a Spirited style.

Considerate Style Body Language. People with a Considerate style generally will make regular but not constant eye contact with you. They have a gentle handshake and are the most likely of all styles to touch an arm or a shoulder. They move more slowly and use smaller gestures when communicating. In the example, Christopher demonstrated a Considerate style.

Systematic Style Body Language. People with a Systematic style generally will make limited eye contact with you. They have a brief handshake and avoid touching otherwise. They move deliberately and use very few gestures when communicating. In our example, Clark displayed a Systematic style.

LISTEN FOR PERSONALITY STYLE CLUES

Another way to identify another person's personality style is to listen carefully. People give you clues through their words and tone of voice. Listen in on these conversations:

Derek is Sally's manager, and Sally supervises Michelle and Don.

Derek (cordially): "Sally, can I share an idea that I think will make you an even better manager? I've noticed that you spend a lot of time in your office with the door closed. I know you're trying to concentrate, but you're giving the impression that you're unavailable to the people on your staff. They don't feel like they can talk to you. I know this because they have come to me instead. And you know me; I'm willing to talk to them. But really, you need to find out what's going on with them and give them the support they need."

Sally (stiffly): "OK, but I'm not going to be all buddy-buddy with them."

Derek (laughing): "You don't have to be—although it couldn't hurt. Just focus on any problems they're encountering, and how you can help resolve them. You're good at that."

Later, Sally calls Michelle into her office.

Sally: "You received my e-mail about establishing regular meeting times with each of my employees. Did you make a list of issues and obstacles you would like to discuss?"

Michelle (concerned): "Is there a problem? I'm not sure why you're asking me for this information all of a sudden."

Sally: "I'm trying to keep everyone's projects organized and on track."

Michelle: "Do you have too much to do? You seem like you're under a lot of pressure. Is there something I can do to help?"

Sally: "No. I have a lot going on, but it's not more than I can handle."

Michelle: "Well, OK. But if you need help, just let me know."

Finally, Sally calls Don into her office.

Sally: "You received my e-mail about—"
Don (curt): "Let me stop you right there. Yes, I received it,
and I can tell you everything is under control."

Direct Style Verbal Communication. People with a Direct style generally use direct language. They say things like, "You must," "You should," or "I want you to." They don't use any hedge phrases, such as "sort of," "kind of," "maybe," or "a little bit." They often jump immediately into the heart of the conversation without making small talk, and they frequently interrupt others. In fact, one of their shortcomings is that they tend to be poor listeners. They express their opinions readily, and they may state their opinions as facts. They speak quickly, and their volume is usually loud. If you find yourself being talked to, rather than engaged in a two-way dialogue, you are probably talking to a Direct individual.

Spirited Style Verbal Communication. People with a Spirited style like to talk. They use enthusiastic and persuasive language, often making sweeping statements and generalizations, and possibly even exaggerations, but you are not likely to hear many details. They like to add exclamations, such as "Wow!," "Fabulous!," "Wonderful!," or "Fantastic!" They express their opinions easily and want you to agree with them. Their conversations tend to go off on tangents and to share a mixture of both personal and work information. If you find yourself listening to a great story, you are probably talking to a Spirited individual.

Considerate Style Verbal Communication. The first thing to notice about people with a Considerate style is that they often listen before they speak. They hesitate to offer their opinions, especially if they believe that doing so will cause conflict or discord. They generally use inclusive language, such as, "What if we . . . ," or "What do you think about . . . ?" They tend to speak more slowly, using a softer voice than people with other styles and pausing more during their conversation. If you find yourself in a conversation where the other person is

Table 3.1 Verbal Communication Differences

	Direct	Spirited	Considerate	Systematic
Type of language used	Uses direct language such as "you must" or "you should"	Uses enthusiastic and persuasive language	Uses inclusive language	Uses precise language
Vocal tendencies	Speaks quickly and loudly	Tendency to exaggerate	Speaks slowly and softly	Speaks with little emotion
Opinions vs. facts	May state opinions as facts	Expresses opinions frequently	Reluctant to offer opinions	Shares facts and data more than opinions
Talking style	Tendency to interrupt others	Talks a lot	Listens before speaking	Has focused conversations
Small talk	Little small talk	Lots of small talk	Lots of small talk	Limited small talk

deferring to your opinion or point of view, you are probably talking to a Considerate person.

Systematic Style Verbal Communication. People with a Systematic style use precise language. They prefer to discuss facts and data rather than opinions and feelings. When they do share their opinions, these will be based on logic and methodical analysis. They tend to speak in a monotone without much vocal variety, and their volume is not too loud or too soft. They don't engage in much small talk or social conversation; their conversations tend to stay focused on the subject at hand. If you find yourself in a conversation that is focused on details and devoid of emotion, you are probably talking to a Systematic individual.

Table 3.1 summarizes the differences among the different communication styles.

EXERCISE: IDENTIFYING PERSONALITY STYLES

Let's revisit Derek, Sally, Michelle, and Don. What insights did you gain from reading about each style? Which personality style would you assign to each person?

Don might be the easiest personality style to figure out. He interrupted his boss and was short and to the point—a Direct style.

Michelle never really revealed her own situation; she simply offered to help Sally, so she probably has a Considerate style.

Sally operated from a very organized, methodical point of view, using few words and little emotion, meaning that she probably has a Systematic style.

Derek talked the most and kept the feedback upbeat, meaning that he probably has a Spirited style.

INTERACT TO IDENTIFY PERSONALITY STYLES

The last way to identify other people's personality styles is to interact with them. There are various ways in which you can do this.

Time Management Clues

You know how some people are always late but end up spending way more time in a meeting than you think is necessary? And how some people are always prompt? Based on what you know about the assertiveness and expressiveness dimensions, you may be able to predict the time management behaviors of each style.

Direct Style Time Management. People with a Direct style don't waste time. They are almost always in a hurry, and they get impatient with you if you aren't. They are action-oriented, making quick decisions and implementing them rapidly. They stay focused on their goals and are seldom tempted to stray off course. If you are working with someone who says, "I want it yesterday!" you are probably working with someone with a Direct style.

Spirited Style Time Management. People with a Spirited style are multitaskers. They enjoy handling a variety of tasks and projects at once, although doing so doesn't necessarily make them more productive. They are easily distracted, finding it much easier to begin a new project than to finish an existing one. They prefer to spend their time brainstorming rather than implementing decisions. If you are working with someone who says, "While we're at it, let's consider . . . ," then you're probably working with someone with a Spirited style.

Considerate Style Time Management. People with a Considerate style put people before time. They will interrupt their own work in order to help others complete their work. They often take on more than they can handle in the interest of helping others—they can't say no! They may also jeopardize their deadlines by not being forceful enough in asking for what they need. If you're working with someone who often asks what he can do to help you, you're probably working with someone with a Considerate style.

Systematic Style Time Management. People with a Systematic style are deadline-driven. You can count on them to meet their deadlines—as long as you give them enough lead time. They often deliberate before making decisions, and they can get bogged down in details. They prefer to spend their time analyzing and evaluating rather than jumping in and taking action on a project. If you're working with someone who seems preoccupied with details and analysis and insists on having enough time to do the job right, then you are probably working with a person with a Systematic style.

Behavior in a Team Clues

Another typical situation in which you interact with others is in a team. Personality styles are evident in the way a team functions. Each style brings specific strengths (and shortcomings) to the team. Not recognizing individual team members' personality styles can create unnecessary obstacles to a team's achieving high performance. For example, if your team needs to make a decision urgently, and you assign a Systematic team member to make that decision on behalf of the team, she might struggle with making a quick decision. Or, if you ask a Spirited team member to be responsible for following through on some routine, detail-oriented activities, that may not happen in a timely manner if you don't give him some oversight. The following descriptions provide additional information about how each personality style is likely to behave in a team.

Direct Style Team Member. If you hear a team member say, "I know what we should do," then you may be working with a Direct style individual. These team members communicate succinctly but assertively. They would rather talk than listen, and they are often the ones who prompt the team to take risks and take action. They are not afraid to engage in conflict, and they usually don't compromise easily. In fact, their shortcomings may also provide clues to their style— they can be critical of other people's ideas and insensitive in how they deliver that criticism. Their impatience and assertiveness can make other team members feel slighted or uncomfortable. Natural team roles for people with the Direct style are Organizer (assigning functions and responsibilities) and Evaluator (monitoring progress and determining accomplishment). See the discussion of team roles in Chapter 7 for more information.

Spirited Style Team Member. If you hear a team member say, "I have a great idea about what we should do," then you may be working with a Spirited style individual. Spirited team members have the most enthusiasm and creative energy of all personality styles. They are fun to be around, and they keep the team's energy and motivation high. On the flip side, their frequent brainstorming can become undisciplined and can cause the team to lose focus, making it difficult for the team to settle on a course of action and move forward to execute it. Spirited style team members will often take on the following roles: Initiator (getting important discussions going and brainstorming ideas) and Encourager (keeping motivation and enthusiasm high).

Considerate Style Team Member. If you hear a team member say, "What do you think we should do?" then you may be working with a Considerate style individual. Considerate style people want to get everyone involved, and they want everyone to get along. If there is a conflict in the team, a Considerate team member is the most likely person to try to resolve it. While these people encourage others to share their ideas, they hesitate to share their own. They are good listeners, and they usually appear to be quieter than other members of the team. As a result, they may seem passive and dependent, and they may be overly sensitive to criticism. A Considerate individual is likely to serve the team as Communicator (keeping everyone in the loop) or Harmonizer (resolving conflict within the team).

Systematic Style Team Member. If you hear a team member say, "Where's the evidence for that?" then you may be working with a Systematic style individual. Such individuals are the most likely team members to organize and assign tasks, set deadlines, and follow through to make sure the work is completed. They will ask many questions in a team meeting, especially related to the details of an issue (rather than the big picture), and they will want time to analyze and evaluate potential decisions and action plans. Because of their perfectionist tendencies, Systematic team members may appear to be overly critical and inflexible. Natural team roles for the Systematic style are Investigator (gathering information and data) and Implementer (following through on the details).

EXERCISE: IDENTIFYING TEAM MEMBERS' PERSONALITY STYLES

Read the following scenario and identify each team member's personality style.

Cary, Adam, Manny, and Grant are team members. Manny is the team leader, and he is reviewing the agenda for their weekly project status meeting.

Manny: "Does anyone have any questions about the agenda?"
Cary: "I don't see the Haven project on the agenda."
Grant: "Why do we still need to discuss that? We decided last week what we were going to do."
Cary: "I was putting the project timeline together, and I saw some issues we didn't figure out yet."
Grant: "I can give you answers."
Manny: "I agree with Grant; I don't want to use our meeting

time to figure out details about the Haven project. We have some new stuff coming up that I want to get your input on."

Adam: "Cary, I can help you put together the timeline outside of the meeting."

Manny: "So, we're agreed. Let's get going on the Forrester proposal."

What is each team member's personality style?

Answers:

Manny: Spirited. He was more interested in talking about new ideas than in reviewing existing projects.

Cary: Systematic. He was focused on organizing the existing project and wanted to have all the details figured out.

Grant: Direct. He was impatient discussing decisions that he thought had already been made.

Adam: Considerate. He didn't provide much input, but he offered to help Cary.

Leadership Behavior Clues

Another way to recognize someone's personality style is to notice how she interacts with you and your coworkers when she is in a leadership role. Note that this doesn't necessarily mean that the person has to be in a management or leadership position; people throughout the ranks of an organization can demonstrate leadership. Depending on their personality styles, individuals will attempt to lead others in significantly different ways.

Direct Style Leadership. Direct style individuals demonstrate leadership by taking charge. They are focused on getting others to achieve results. You will notice them telling others what to do, urging people to take action, and being focused on the goal. They provide candid (some would say blunt) feedback to others, and they offer solutions rather than solicit input when they are interacting with others.

Spirited Style Leadership. Spirited style individuals demonstrate leadership by inspiring others. They are focused on persuading people to get behind a common vision. You will notice them motivating and energizing others, creating excitement that makes others want to join with them, and painting a picture of possibilities that encourages others to want to do their best. They interact with others by cheerleading and giving recognition.

Considerate Style Leadership. Considerate style individuals demonstrate leadership by building group harmony. They are focused on increasing organization performance by building team cohesiveness. You will notice them involving others by asking for their input, listening carefully, and offering support. They strive to create a comfortable work environment that makes it easy for people to complete their work. In other words, they try to remove obstacles that hinder getting work done, and, in their minds, conflict is one of those obstacles. They interact with others with patience and empathy.

Systematic Style Leadership. Systematic style individuals demonstrate leadership by planning and organizing information and people. They are focused on improving the organization by increasing its quality, accuracy, and productivity. You will notice them urging others to achieve and maintain the highest standards of quality and performance, and using data to drive decisions and actions throughout the organization. They interact with others in a straightforward way, focusing on the work at hand without engaging in much small talk or socializing.

 ## Exercise: Identifying Personality Styles in a Leadership Role

Read the following scenario and see if you can identify the personality styles of each of the people that Malcolm mentions.

> Malcolm is reflecting on people he has worked with who demonstrated leadership.
>
> "Doug is the first person who comes to mind. He was my first boss, and he was straight out of a textbook—you know, very authoritative and powerful. This was back in the days when we still wore ties to work, and he always wore a suit. He

didn't have a lot to say, but with just a few words, he gave you the direction you needed, and you always wanted to achieve the best results for him.

"Then I think of Caroline, because she was almost the exact opposite of Doug, but she was effective in her own way. She was the VP of HR, and she was perfect in that role. She was soft spoken and caring, and she made people feel comfortable from the first day they started. She showed her leadership skills by somehow enabling this diverse group of people to pull together and work together to achieve a common good.

"Jackie was a leader, but it wasn't obvious. Instead of being the visible leader out front, she was more in the background. But her drive to achieve high standards kept us all motivated to do the same. She expected the best, and she didn't accept anything less. She was like the teacher in school who was really strict, but deep down you liked her a lot.

"Richard is the most memorable character I've worked with. He was kind of like the Pied Piper—his enthusiasm was infectious, and people just wanted to be around him. Even when his ideas weren't the greatest, people would support him. So he was our leader, but he didn't always lead us in the best direction."

Based on the information you've learned, what personality style is each of the people Malcolm mentioned?

Answers:

Doug: Direct

Caroline: Considerate

Jackie: Systematic

Richard: Spirited

Recognizing Styles in a Virtual or Remote World

Because of advances in technology, more and more employees find themselves working from home or working with colleagues who keep different hours, work in different offices, or are even in different parts of the world. When you are interacting with people remotely, you don't have the advantage of face-to-face clues to identify their personality styles. Instead, you have to rely on written words in e-mails and texts, and on words and tone of voice in phone conversations. Although it may take a bit longer and require careful sleuthing, you still can determine their personality styles accurately.

Direct style individuals are likely to have short and to the point communications, both their phone conversations and their e-mails. In conversations, these people are more likely to talk *at* you than *with* you. They will jump directly into the topic at hand, speak quickly, and hang up when they are through. When you send them an e-mail that doesn't require a response, don't expect one. And don't be offended by a lack of salutation at the beginning or end of a message; it's just their style.

Spirited style individuals are likely to be long-winded, both in their e-mails and in their phone conversations. Conversations, in particular, are likely to drift off topic, but they will be lively and interesting. You are likely to end up being on the phone with a Spirited colleague for a lot longer than you expected. When you send an e-mail, you may not hear back from a Spirited individual in a timely manner—but she will be apologetic when she finally does get back to you.

Considerate style individuals will often begin e-mails and conversations with "small talk"—asking how your day is going, or how your weekend was, for example. In a phone call, they will engage you in conversation and ask you questions to get your opinions. They are great listeners, so you may find yourself talking more than usual. The pace and tone will be relaxed and casual. When you send them an e-mail that doesn't require a response, they are likely to respond anyway, with a "thanks" or "let me know if I can help."

Systematic style individuals are likely to write detailed e-mails, probably containing bulleted lists. They will provide information in an organized and logical manner, and they are unlikely to add any social niceties—casual conversation unrelated to the topic. They will follow a similar pattern in phone conversations. You may feel as if there are long silences in the conversation and you've lost their attention, but they are probably considering their response and are less aware of the silence than you are (if you don't have a Systematic style yourself).

EXERCISE: RECOGNIZING PERSONALITY STYLES IN E-MAILS

Based on the information you just learned, read each e-mail and decide the personality style of the sender.

1. _____

Subject: Great idea!

Hi Sam,

I was talking to Frank in Shipping, and he mentioned that their budget proposal was accepted as submitted, without any reductions. I think we can swipe some great ideas from them. Stop by my office and we'll discuss. Thanks for your help with this!

2. _____

Subject: Budget reformat

Sam, as I reviewed the budget proposal, several thoughts came to mind:

- Highlight positive aspects of each option.
- Minimize duplication of information.
- Copy last year's format to save time.

Let me know if you can move ahead, or if you need additional information.

3. _____

Subject: What do you think?

Hi Sam,

How's it going? I was working on revising the budget proposal and thought we might want to emphasize the positive aspects of the various options more. I can work on some different formats if you think it's a good idea. Let me know your thoughts.

4. _____

Subject: Budget reformat

We need to reformat the budget options to highlight the positive aspects of each and minimize duplication of information. See what I did in last year's proposal for direction. Budget is due on Friday. Let me know if you have any questions.

Answers:

1. Spirited

2. Systematic

3. Considerate

4. Direct

Table 3.2 serves as a summary of clues to identifying personality styles.

Table 3.2   **Clues to Personality Styles**

Category/clue	Direct	Spirited	Considerate	Systematic
Assertiveness	High	High	Low	Low
Expressiveness	Low	High	High	Low
Pace	Quick	Quick	Slow	Slow
Priorities	Taking action, getting results	Persuading others, gaining recognition	Giving support, maintaining harmony	Ensuring quality and accuracy
Motivated by	Power, authority, competition, success, winning	Social recognition	Appreciation, cooperation	Gaining expertise and knowledge
Strengths	Confidence, risk taking	Enthusiasm, ability to persuade	Patience, good listener	Accuracy, logical/rational thinking
Shortcomings	Impatience and insensitivity	Impulsiveness and disorganization	Indecisiveness, overly accommodating	Overly critical, tendency to overanalyze
Fears	Loss of control	Rejection, loss of influence	Disapproval, offending others, change	Being wrong

▶ POINTS TO REMEMBER

- ▶ Recognize personality styles by observation.
  - Desk test
    - Organized piles = Direct
    - Messy = Spirited
    - Personal mementos = Considerate
    - Tidy = Systematic
  - Learning styles
    - Independent, active/doing = Direct
    - Group, active/doing = Spirited
    - Group, thinking/reflecting = Considerate
    - Independent, thinking/reflecting = Systematic
  - Body language
    - Forceful gestures = Direct
    - Animated gestures = Spirited
    - Touching gestures = Considerate
    - Limited and controlled gestures = Systematic
- ▶ Recognize personality styles by listening.
  - Direct verbal communication: loud, fast, and direct Talk more than listen.
  - Spirited verbal communication: long-winded and enthusiastic
  - Considerate verbal communication: soft-spoken, casual Listen more than talk.
  - Systematic verbal communication: to the point, focused on facts.

▶ Recognize personality styles by interacting.

- Time management behaviors
  - Don't waste time = Direct
  - Multitaskers = Spirited
  - Put people before time = Considerate
  - Deadline-driven = Systematic
- Team behaviors
  - Like to take charge = Direct
  - Like to brainstorm = Spirited
  - Like to support = Considerate
  - Like to complete = Systematic
- Leadership behaviors
  - Telling others = Direct
  - Inspiring others = Spirited
  - Supporting others = Considerate
  - Urging others to high standards = Systematic

▶ Recognize personality styles in a high-technology world.

- Direct e-mail: short; don't expect a response if none is required.
- Spirited e-mail: long-winded; don't expect a timely response.
- Considerate e-mail: starts with small talk; expect a response to every e-mail.
- Systematic e-mail: detailed; bulleted lists.

Four

WHEN STYLES COLLIDE

n this chapter, we'll look at different types of conflict, the reasons for each type, how to resolve each of them, and how to handle conflict when people with different styles are stressed out.

> Isabelle and Jack were talking in the break room. Jack asked Isabelle, "What did you think of the meeting?" Isabelle paused for a moment and then responded, "The agenda was well organized, but we didn't stick to it. We got off topic, and I'm not sure the decision we reached was thought through enough—I'm already seeing some problems when we try to implement it." Jack was surprised and disappointed. "Wow, that was harsh. Why don't you tell me how you really feel?" he said sarcastically. Isabelle said, "Well, you asked." Jack replied, "Yes, but I thought you'd say it was great, or at least that you liked the skit." Isabelle said, "The skit? Please don't do that again."

This is a classic example of two personality styles clashing. As you have inferred, Isabelle is a detail-oriented Systematic, whereas Jack has a Spirited style; he generalizes and cares about keeping people entertained. When two people clash, it can be for a variety of reasons.

TYPES OF CONFLICT

Not all conflicts are the same. Some conflicts are deeply divisive and can cause permanent rifts in relationships, whereas other conflicts are more superficial and transitory. The good news is that most conflicts are resolvable, and perhaps can even be avoided in the first place.

The most serious conflicts are values-based, where a difference in values cannot be resolved easily.[1] When the conflict arises from differing concepts of what is right and wrong, or good and bad, then it becomes difficult to identify any shared purpose or goal, and reasoning, negotiation, and problem solving are unlikely to have any positive results.

A second type of conflict is issues-based. These are conflicts that involve ideas, actions, decisions, policies, and other such matters. They can usually be dealt with through rational problem solving that can lead to productive and creative solutions.

The last type of conflict is style-based. These conflicts are usually about perceived negative attitudes, behaviors, and motives. They have a way of growing over time if left unheeded.

To determine whether a conflict is style-based, ask yourself the following questions:

- Do I become quickly frustrated when dealing with this person?

- Do I want to "win"?

- Are my emotions related to this conflict out of balance with its importance?

- Do I find other issues to argue about when I'm dealing with this person?

If you answered yes to any of these questions, you are dealing with a style-based conflict, at least in part. Let's look at how the styles typically match up and the most common areas of conflict for each pair.

STYLE COMPATIBILITY AND CLASHES

You will recall that the two dimensions of personality style are assertiveness and expressiveness. In general, tension is least likely to occur along a shared dimension and most likely to occur when the dimensions are not shared. Let's look at each style combination as it relates to compatibility and conflict.

Direct/Spirited. People with this style combination are likely to get along and develop rapport based on their mutual assertive natures;

however, they may run into trouble if they sense that a competition is developing. When this happens, they may become overly demanding of each other. They will both be focused on achievement; however, the Direct is looking for business results, while the Spirited is more interested in social success.

Spirited/Considerate. The Spirited and Considerate styles are both high in expressiveness, and people with these styles are likely to develop an easy rapport. In addition, people with the Considerate style are naturally supportive of everyone, so this combination has the potential to be a very smooth-running relationship. The greatest potential for conflict is an energy clash, where the Spirited person's enthusiasm and constant commotion may overwhelm and then frustrate the Considerate person.

Considerate/Systematic. This combination shares space on the assertiveness dimension (low) but is dissimilar on the expressiveness dimension. The result? The Considerate person will probably talk too much for the Systematic person's preference, and the Systematic person may get irritated with what he perceives as the Considerate person's wasting time. They can work well together, but since both styles are on the low end of the assertiveness dimension, they may have trouble making firm decisions and moving a project forward. Instead, they may get stuck in discussions and analyses.

Systematic/Direct. The Systematic and Direct styles share space on the expressiveness dimension (low), so their communication styles are similar. Neither style feels the need to be especially concerned with the other's feelings. However, their work styles are very different, and that is where tension is likely to occur. Someone with a Direct style moves much faster than someone with a Systematic style and is likely to become frustrated with the slower pace of a Systematic person's decision-making process. On the other hand, the Systematic person is likely to become unhappy with the Direct person's apparent knee-jerk decisions and lack of thoughtful analysis.

Direct/Considerate. People with this combination are opposite on both the assertiveness and expressiveness dimensions, so they may struggle to develop rapport with each other. The Considerate person values time spent together, whereas someone with the Direct style doesn't share this value. And someone with the Direct style values decisive, authoritative action, whereas someone with the Considerate style values inclusiveness and consensus in decision making. However, their strengths complement each other, and they can be effective in accomplishing tasks and projects together, even though they may not bond with each other.

Spirited/Systematic. This combination is also diametrically opposed, and the people involved may get frustrated with each other and have trouble developing rapport. Someone with a Spirited style develops rapport by talking first, while someone with the Systematic style develops rapport by doing first—working together. The person with the Spirited style may get exasperated by the Systematic person's demand for order and a methodical, logical approach to work. Meanwhile, the Systematic person may get irritated by what she perceives as the Spirited person's haphazard way of working.

Same/Same

What happens when two people share the same style? In most cases, they are likely to get along well because they have much in common in terms of how they communicate and how they approach their work. However, that is not true in every case.

Direct/Direct. Because of the nature of the Direct style, two Direct style people working together may clash because they both want to be in charge and want their own way. Friendly competition may quickly escalate to a serious desire to beat the other person and win.

Spirited/Spirited. People with this combination are likely to enjoy each other's company and get along well. However, when it comes to getting work done, each may want the other to handle the details; they will both resist and may reach a stalemate, delaying the task or project and creating ill will.

Considerate/Considerate. These two will get along well and will be very supportive of each other. However, if they are working on a task together, one is going to have to take the lead, and their reluctance to take charge may hinder progress on the task or project.

Systematic/Systematic. These two will work well together. They will organize their work and divvy up assignments evenly. They may not become fast friends, but they are unlikely to rub each other the wrong way.

 ### Exercise: Applying Styles to Project Management

Put this knowledge into practice by looking at the typical life cycle of a project.[2] Think about which style combinations might work well together and which styles might clash at each phase of the project.

Phase 1: Initiation. In this stage, you meet and brainstorm to define the project and develop goals and outcomes. Often, you need to develop a business case for the project.

Styles that would collaborate: _____

_____

Styles that would collide: _____

_____

Phase 2: Planning. This stage involves creating a plan with an overall schedule, identification of individual tasks, allocation of resources (time, money, and people), and assignment of deliverables, with deadlines and specific criteria for the completion of each deliverable.

Styles that would collaborate: _____

_____

Styles that would collide: _____

_____

Phase 3: Implementation. This is the stage in which you do the work, monitor the work, and deal with performance issues, resources issues (not enough!), and changes in scope.

Styles that would collaborate: _____

_____

Styles that would collide: _____

Phase 4: Evaluation. In the final stage, you wrap up the project with a review and analysis of what went well and what didn't, and make any final adjustments so that the project can be closed out successfully.

Styles that would collaborate: _____

Styles that would collide: _____

Ideas to Think About

Phase 1: Initiation. Since this is a stage that involves brainstorming, two Spirited project members will collaborate well together. A Spirited/Direct combination might also generate some big ideas. On the other hand, a Spirited/Systematic combination might clash because the Systematic would already be looking ahead to implementation issues—in other words, the Spirited would be seeing the forest, while the Systematic would be looking at the trees.

Phase 2: Planning. A Direct paired with a Systematic or a Considerate would work well in the planning stage. But two Directs working together might clash if they don't see precisely eye to eye; each would want his own way, and they might argue over details. A Considerate/Systematic combination might not clash with each other, but it may not be the best combination to move the project forward because people with both styles are slow decision makers.

Phase 3: Implementation. Two Systematic project members will work well together in this stage, when many decisions have already been made and it's time for the work to be carried out. Considerates will be a calming influence, and Directs will keep things moving along. If someone with the Spirited style is paired with people with any other style, this may cause friction if the Spirited person fails to meet deadlines or complete her assignments. Someone with the Spirited style may also try to change the scope of the project in midstream. This will especially bother a Systematic person.

Phase 4: Evaluation. The Systematic style paired with the Spirited style could work well in this stage if the Systematic person is allowed to lead with his analysis, and then the Spirited person could help brainstorm ways to improve. A Direct/Systematic combination may clash if the Direct person jumps to conclusions without thoroughly reviewing the analysis.

CONFLICT STYLES

Each style has its own typical approach to conflict. These tips will help you work with people with each style in a typical, nonescalated conflict (see Figure 4.1). Later in the chapter, we'll look at how to handle people with each style when they are feeling stressed and under pressure.

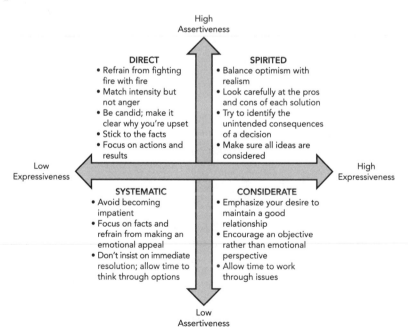

Figure 4.1 **Tips for Dealing with Each Style in a Conflict**

Direct Style. People with a Direct style address conflict head-on, to the point where they may become argumentative or belligerent. They will interrupt others and increase the volume and intensity of their voices if they feel they aren't being heard. They value honesty, but not tact. Others may see them as difficult to work with when they are at their worst in a conflict.

How do you work through conflict when you are dealing with someone with a Direct style? Refrain from fighting fire with fire. Match the person's intensity, but not her anger. Be candid and make it clear why you're upset, but stick to the facts and focus on actions and results.

Spirited Style. People with a Spirited style are not afraid to tackle conflict directly, and they don't hesitate to share their feelings about the situation. In fact, they may monopolize the conversation and become overly dramatic. Others may feel overwhelmed or manipulated by the Spirited person's emotions in the midst of the conflict.

How do you work through conflict when you are dealing with someone with a Spirited style? Balance optimism with realism—look carefully at the pros and cons of each proposed solution before deciding on the best one. In particular, look at the potential unintended consequences of the solution you're considering. Avoid letting the Spirited person's persuasive skills overwhelm or drown out others' ideas.

Considerate Style. People with a Considerate style usually want to avoid conflict at all costs. They are likely to give in easily in order to avoid a confrontation. Although they are concerned with other people's feelings, they are unlikely to reveal their own feelings or opinions about the situation. This may lead others to conclude that the Considerate person is weak or is uninterested in working through the conflict.

How do you work through conflict when you are dealing with someone with a Considerate style? Emphasize your desire to maintain a good relationship. Emphasize that success (resolution) will be achieved more quickly by focusing on the issue objectively rather than emotionally. Allow time for the Considerate person to work through his cautious nature to reach a solution that he feels comfortable with.

Systematic Style. People with a Systematic style are likely to become entrenched in their position when there is a conflict. They will stick to the facts and may get uncomfortable with other people's emotions. Others may perceive them as rigid, insensitive, and unwilling to compromise in a conflict.

How do you work through conflict when you are dealing with someone with a Systematic style? Avoid becoming impatient or reacting too emotionally. Focus on facts rather than on an emotional appeal for your desired solution. Don't insist on immediate resolution; give her time to process the situation.

CONFRONTATION MODEL FOR ADDRESSING STYLE-BASED CONFLICT

If you find yourself in a style-based conflict, it is important that you acknowledge it and address it. Just ignoring it usually causes frustration and makes subsequent interactions more challenging and disagreeable. Follow these steps to diplomatically and objectively address the conflict.[3]

CONFRONTATION MODEL

1. State your observations.

2. State your emotions.

3. Request the behavior you want.

First, state your observations. Describe the other person's behavior in specific terms, for example, "When I asked you a question, you crossed your arms and rolled your eyes." Avoid making general statements with labels or judgments, such as, "You acted like I'm an idiot." Those with a Systematic style will be able to do this naturally, while those with the other styles will have to make a conscious effort to be objective.

Next, state your emotions, taking ownership of how you feel, for example, "I felt embarrassed." Avoid expressing emotions that lay blame on the other person, such as, "I felt you were mocking me."

In addition, provide context by stating your reasons for your emotions, for example, "I felt embarrassed because I sensed that people were judging me." In this step, people with the Direct style may be prone to using blaming language (for example, "You always . . ."). People with the Spirited style may use exaggeration, which can make it difficult to identify their true feelings. And those with the Considerate and Systematic styles may have trouble expressing their feelings at all.

Finally, request the behavior you want. Make sure you express this in terms of what you want, not what you don't want. Once again, make it specific and action oriented. So, saying, "Quit yelling at me," or, "Be more supportive," is ineffective. Instead, say, "Please keep your voice low," or, "Please share your concerns with me in private." Being positive is a strength of the Spirited style, while people with the Systematic and Direct styles may need to work at phrasing their requests in a positive manner. Those with the Considerate style may struggle with stating their needs at all.

Keep in mind that confronting the other person doesn't guarantee a change in her behavior. After all, it can be difficult to change! It gives you the opportunity to state your concerns in a positive way, but you need to realize that the outcome might not go the way you want.

Resolving Issues-Based Conflict

The following is an example of a heated discussion that resulted from competing issues:

> Andrew, a salesperson, and Maria, the shipping department manager, were having a heated discussion. Andrew said, "One of my best customers called and said that his shipment didn't arrive when it was promised. When I looked into it, I was told that the shipping department was understaffed when his order was supposed to go out, so it was delayed. How am I going to keep my customers if you guys can't keep up the level of customer service they expect?" Maria responded, "It's not that simple. Our budget for labor costs was cut in order to maintain

our profitability. We can't afford to hire temps every time someone calls in sick." Andrew said, "Well, you need to come up
with something else, because if I lose sales over this, you won't
have any profit anyway!"

When conflicts are based on substantive issues, you need to use rational problem solving to produce constructive solutions. In order
to be effective, you must address the conflict in a way that takes the
emotion out of it and allows you and the other person to focus on the
issue.[4] Follow these strategies to help ensure success.

First, bring the issue to the other person's attention in a way that
will engage him rather than cause him to get defensive. Managing the
emotions around the conflict is critical to reaching a successful resolution. In general, you want to convey curiosity instead of accusation,
be open-minded and flexible, and approach the discussion as a two-
way conversation. Here's an example of a conversation opener that
doesn't work with anyone: "We need to talk." This sounds harmless,
but assuming that it's expressed with a stern tone of voice and rigid
body language, it sounds as if the receiver will be talked *at* instead of
with, and it will immediately put the other person on the defensive.
In general, a safe approach is to ask a general, open-ended question
that will open the conversation.

When approaching a Direct, try asking, "What obstacles do you
see that are getting in the way of meeting our goals for this project?"

When approaching a Spirited, try asking, "What ideas do you
have for how to improve the way this project is going?"

When approaching a Considerate, try asking, "How do you feel
we could support each other better on this project?"

When approaching a Systematic, try asking, "If there is one thing
you could change to improve the way we work together on this project, what would it be?"

Next, you want to gain agreement on the nature of the conflict.
This involves defining the problem and agreeing on the desired outcome. In this step, it's critical that you identify the root cause, not
merely the symptom. Recognize that it's possible that there may be
more than one issue wrapped up in the conflict. Systematics will
be skilled at this step, whereas Spariteds will resist taking the time to

examine an issue in depth, and Directs may jump to conclusions. In addition, people with the Spirited and Considerate styles may perceive the conflict as being based on personal issues because they feel emotional about it. They need extra help separating the issues from their emotions.

Once you have defined the problem and both sides are in agreement about what the problem is, then you can move to finding a solution. Instead of getting attached to a certain position, stay focused on the positive outcome you are trying to achieve, and be flexible about the means to achieve it. As you can imagine, this is the forte of people with the Spirited style, whereas Systematics and Considerates may have trouble imagining new solutions or new ways of doing things. And Directs may just want it their way and get entrenched in their position.

Avoid offering options that you know will be unacceptable to the other person. On the other hand, remain open and flexible yourself—consider options as starting points, not as final agreements. Resolving issues-based conflicts usually involves compromise. You may not get everything you want, but the solution should be acceptable and should meet your common goal.

Implement the solution. For Systematics, this may be the easiest part of the conflict resolution process, whereas for Spiriteds, it may be the most difficult. Put your agreement in writing. Be specific about actions, behaviors, and associated time frames. Agree on consequences for noncompliance, and put those in writing, too. This sounds harsh, but it provides an objective document that you can refer to if the conflict should arise again or if it is not resolved the way you discussed and agreed on. Follow up and express your confidence that you and the other person can continue to work together effectively.

As mentioned at the beginning of this chapter, values-based conflicts are the most difficult to resolve. Some are impossible. People don't want to compromise their deeply held beliefs. But you can maintain a good working relationship with someone even when you have deep-seated disagreements. The key is to find another shared value on which to base your relationship. And that usually involves spending time with the other person to get to know her as an individual, even when your instinct is to avoid her.

WHEN CONFLICT ESCALATES

In some cases, despite your best efforts (or perhaps because of your lack of effort), the conflict may escalate. Here are some signs that the conflict is escalating: you start moving from a mindset of rational self-interest to getting even, you begin seeing only what's wrong with the other person, the conflict widens from one specific issue to many issues or to general complaints, or you try to enlist others on your side of the conflict. All four styles can escalate conflicts, although these may become visible in different ways.

People with the high-assertiveness styles, Direct and Spirited, are more likely to exhibit physical, visible signs of escalation: they raise their voices, their tone of voice becomes strident, their muscles get tense, and they experience abrupt mood shifts. Also, when people with these styles observe these behaviors in the other person, their instinct will be to match them and become combative themselves.

People with the low-assertiveness styles, Considerate and Systematic, are more likely to exhibit escalation by increasing resentment, engaging in gossip (Considerates), or complaining more (Systematics).

Another symptom of escalation is that your language changes. You start blaming the other person or trying to make him look bad, for example, "I wouldn't have had to tell him if you had told me sooner." It is also common for people to begin generalizing or exaggerating for example, "You can't stand to be wrong," or, "You never listen to me."

To deescalate a conflict, basically, you need to do the opposite. Lower your volume, relax your muscles, and take a deep breath. Avoid "absolutes" and use words such as "maybe," "what if," "perhaps," or, "sometimes," for example, "I've noticed several occasions when . . ." Think about asking open-ended questions, for example, "What are your thoughts about . . . ?"

Respect the other person's feelings as being real to her and let her vent. If the other person is worked up and emotional, it will be impossible to have a productive conversation. Obviously, the same is true if you are overly emotional. Therefore, your goal is to help drain excessive emotions so that both of you can express your feelings in a constructive way.

One way to do that is to show empathy. Let the other person know that you can imagine being in his shoes by saying something like, "I can appreciate your perspective." People with the Considerate style are naturally skilled at showing empathy. Refocus on your common goal or desired outcome by asking, "What is the real issue here?" or "What do we want to accomplish?" Resist the urge to bring up the past or other issues that are bothering you. Patience is key!

Since patience is a key ingredient in deescalating a conflict, you can guess which style will have to work hardest at this—the Direct style is not wired with a great deal of patience.

Dealing with Styles Under Stress

When people with each style are under stress and feeling pressured, their trouble spots may intensify and become extreme. This makes them challenging to work with and makes any conflict even more difficult to resolve. We'll look at each of these "stressed" personalities and offer strategies for dealing with each one.

The Direct Under Stress

When people with the Direct style are extremely stressed in a conflict situation, they can become hot-tempered. At their worst, they lose their cool and blow up at others, use exaggerated gestures, and often blame others. The problem is that they often return to this strategy because it has been successful in the past—it has gotten them what they wanted.

> Derek has just found out that a coworker, Susan, asked for and received permission to attend a specialized training session being held in another state. He confronts his supervisor, Ann. "This is blatant favoritism. You have always liked Susan better than me, and this proves it," he says. Ann replies, "Derek, we have a limited budget, and Susan's experience makes her a better candidate to attend this training." Derek says, "That's baloney. I'm not going to let this go! I'm taking it up with HR, and you'll be sorry!"

The first step in dealing with a stressed-out Direct is to repeat to yourself, "It's not about me." Of course, it will be difficult for you not to take it personally, but you have to remember that a stressed-out person with the Direct style lashes out at anyone. And looking at it from a positive point of view, you know where you stand, and the Direct is getting it out of his system and is unlikely to backstab later.

One surprising technique to try is to ask for more, literally asking, "Is there anything else?" If you can do this using a noncritical (and not sarcastic!) tone of voice, it can be effective in breaking the pattern of the stressed-out Direct person. If he shows no sign of backing off, you can try switching to an "automatic" response. Choose a statement such as, "I want to have a productive conversation, but I can't do that when you're yelling," and keep repeating it. Set clear boundaries, such as, "This is important to me, and I will continue this conversation as soon as you can talk without yelling." It is important that you follow through on whatever consequences you have set. For example, you may need to walk away until the stressed-out Direct person calms down.

Finally, find agreement about something for example, "I can see that this is important to you; it's important to me, too," or, "I know we can work through this."

The Spirited Under Stress

When people with the Spirited style feel stressed, they tend to intensify their verbal behavior and take it to an extreme. They may respond to criticism and conflict with verbal attacks and persist in trying to convince others to adopt their point of view. They may act impulsively, and they may be sarcastic or take shots at people with comments veiled as jokes. They may even blow up when they feel unappreciated.

> Andrew and Caroline are high school teachers who are meeting about choosing a new textbook for the science department. Andrew mentions that the principal thought the current textbook was one of the worst she had ever seen. Caroline is upset. "I chose that textbook. She doesn't know what she's

talking about. I'm going to give her a piece of my mind!" Andrew is shocked: "Whoa, Caroline. Back off. I don't know any of the details about why she said that, and it's certainly not a knock against you."

Respond to a stressed-out person with a Spirited style by calling her on her remarks. Use a neutral, calm tone of voice, and don't be nasty in return. For example, you can say, "I like working with you, and this is an important issue to discuss. However, when you put me down like you just did, I lose my motivation to work together."

Try to head off an outburst by using the person's name and reminding her that she will be sorry for hurting people's feelings (because she will regret it). You can say, "Julie, stop and listen to yourself. I know you care too much about our relationship to treat me this way." Of course, make sure that your own tone of voice is neutral, not critical, and that your body language is calm, not tense. Your goal is to help the other person gain control over her actions, words, and emotions.

The Considerate Under Stress

As you know, people with the Considerate style avoid conflict. Their instinct is to sweep it under the rug and ignore it as much as possible. They may do this by using stalling tactics, such as canceling a meeting or asking for more time to work on a project. Or they may use outright avoidance, simply denying that anything is wrong.

> Richard and Claire were working together, and Richard noticed that Claire was very quiet. Richard asked, "What's wrong?" Claire said, "Nothing's wrong." Richard responded, "Well, you're acting like you're mad at me." Claire said, "I told you, nothing's wrong." Richard dropped it, but later in the break room he overhead Claire telling a coworker that she was upset because Richard had given her only an average rating on her 360° performance appraisal.

Dealing with someone who refuses to acknowledge a conflict can be very frustrating. Ironically for Considerates, avoiding conflict has the opposite effect from what they want—instead of developing close, supportive relationships, they will end up with superficial relationships in which there is a lack of meaningful trust and support.

To deal with someone who avoids conflict, use gentle confrontation. If you have a high-assertiveness style (Direct or Spirited), be conscious of your usual high energy and quick pace, and be prepared to slow down and be patient. Soften your tone of voice, your body language, and your choice of words. Acknowledge that the topic may be difficult to discuss. Make the conflict appear small and manageable, for example, "Let's look at one thing that will make our relationship run more smoothly." Allow time for the Considerate to think about his response—this may mean coming back together a day or so later to return to the discussion.

Be sure to provide positive feedback about all that is going well. Express appreciation for the aspects of the relationship that are successful. If you are a low-expressiveness style (Systematic or Direct), you may have to use more self-disclosure than you are typically comfortable with in order to build rapport and trust with the Considerate conflict avoider. Lighten up the situation with a smile, an affectionate gesture, or even some humor—sincere and appropriate, not sarcastic or hurtful.

People who avoid conflict usually just want to help others and not make trouble, so show them how dealing with the issue is a way of helping, or how not dealing with the issue is actually unhelpful. For example, "If I have overlooked a problem with this new system and you don't share your concerns about it, then I'm not able to make it better for everyone."

The Systematic Under Stress

When they are stressed out in a conflict situation, Systematics may become uncooperative. This may stem from a lack of confidence about the situation and a desire to fall back on what makes them feel comfortable, which is withdrawing from others and delaying decision making, and that can be seen by others as being uncooperative.

Mary, a salesperson, asked Samantha, the IT manager, to help her prepare a proposal for a potential new and large client that is in the IT industry. Samantha refused. "If I help you, then I need to help anyone else who asks me, and I don't have time to do that." Mary was distressed. "Samantha, this could be the client that helps the company make its sales quota for the quarter." Samantha was adamant: "Sales is your job, not mine."

Often, the underlying reason behind a lack of cooperation is a fear of change. Resolving conflict involves a change of some sort, and people with the Systematic style prefer known routines and procedures to unknown ones. Help the uncooperative person feel more comfortable with change by explaining how the current situation is preventing you, your department, or the organization from achieving its highest potential for success. Explain how coming up with a new solution will maintain the high standards that the uncooperative person wants to maintain.

To resolve conflict with an uncooperative person, avoid attacking her position or point of view. Let her know that you understand her interests, and tie those interests to yours. For example, "I know you don't want to compromise on this because you want to maintain the highest standards for the organization. So do I. So let's stop for a minute and refocus on what we agree on." Try to overcome the person's resistance by explaining the specific benefit to her of resolving the conflict.

Get the person involved in the solution—don't dictate terms. Ask the person to describe the outcome she wants and how she would achieve it. Help her see that she's not a helpless bystander in the situation, and that you aren't out to get her or make her miserable.

Exercise: Dealing with Conflict

Describe a conflict you are currently dealing with or have recently dealt with at work.

What type of conflict is it: values-based, issues-based, or style-based? How can you tell?

If it is values-based, what other value do you and the other person share that you could base your relationship on?

If it is issues-based, how could you approach problem solving with the other person, based on his personality style, to engage him in resolving the conflict?

If it is style-based, how can you adjust your style to communicate and work with the other person more effectively?

▶ POINTS TO REMEMBER

- ▶ Types of conflict
  - • Values-based
  - • Issues-based
  - • Personality-based

- ▶ Style compatibility and clashes. In general, styles are compatible when they share space on a dimension (assertiveness or expressiveness) and clash when they are on opposite ends of a dimension.

- ▶ Conflict styles
  - • *Direct:* Addresses conflict head-on. Work with such people by matching their intensity but not their anger.

  - • *Spirited:* Expresses feelings dramatically. Handle such people by balancing optimism with realism and avoiding being overly influenced by their persuasive skills.

  - • *Considerate:* Avoids conflict at all costs. Work with such people by showing support and allowing time for them to get comfortable expressing their needs.

  - • *Systematic:* Relies on facts and not emotions. Handle conflict with such people by restraining your own emotion and allowing time for them to consider potential solutions.

▶ Confrontation model

- State your observations.

- State your emotions.

- Request the behavior you want.

▶ Resolving issues-based conflict

- Engage the other person.

- Identify and agree on the problem.

- Find a solution that meets your common interests.

- Implement the solution.

▶ Dealing with styles under stress

- *The Direct under stress:* To handle such a person, remember that it's not about you. Set clear boundaries.

- *The Spirited under stress:* To handle such a person, interrupt the person's outburst and help her gain control over her words and emotions.

- *The Considerate under stress:* To handle such a person, use gentle confrontation. Make it safe for him to express his needs and feelings.

- *The Systematic under stress:* To handle such a person, help her overcome her resistance to change.

PART III

PERSONALITY STYLE IN THE REAL WORLD— A STYLE FOR EVERY SITUATION

Five

STYLES AND
COMMUNICATION

H ave you ever tried communicating with someone who speaks a different language from yours? You can convey a few thoughts with gestures and perhaps some similar words, but it is nearly impossible to understand completely or be understood.

> Brian is waiting for Rachael—again. Finally, Rachael arrives for the meeting, sits down, and begins chitchatting. She asks Brian, "How was your weekend? Did you do anything fun? Do you have a busy week coming up?" Brian is clearly irritated. "Why are you asking me all these questions? We're running late as it is." Rachael responds, "I was just trying to be nice."

THE THREE-STEP COMMUNICATION PROCESS

Communication is both simple and complex at the same time. Simple, but not easy. At its essence, one person sends a message, and the other person receives it. The trick is making sure that the message that is received is the same as the one that the sender intended. To increase the odds for success, think of communication as happening in three steps:[1]

> Prepare yourself and the other person.
>
> Send your message.
>
> Check for understanding.

We'll look at each step in detail. Keep in mind that we will be focusing primarily on face-to-face communication that is work related. Just shooting the breeze doesn't require the same attention to structure and effort (although it can't hurt).

Prepare Yourself and the Other Person

The first step in the communication process is to prepare yourself and the other person. Some aspects of preparing yourself happen automatically or instinctively, and other parts require conscious effort. First, you need to know your purpose. If you have a Direct style, you are probably thinking, "Well, of course!" right now. If you have a Spirited style, you may be thinking, "My purpose is to talk." That's not what we mean. Knowing your purpose means knowing what you want to say and why you want to say it. Generally, there are three purposes to communication, and they roughly correspond to three of the personality styles.

> *To inform.* This approach is frequently associated with a Direct or Systematic style. Here's an example: "We are at 98 percent of our monthly budget allowance for office supplies with 10 days left in the month. We need to stop any further purchases immediately."

> *To persuade.* This purpose is characteristic of the Spirited style. Here's an example: "Frank, I know cash is tight, but we need more money. Our department size has doubled, but not our budget."

> *To inquire.* This purpose is typical of a Considerate style. Here's an example: "What do you think we can do to avoid overspending on our office supply budget this month, and in the future?"

After you determine your purpose, decide what outcome you desire. What do you want the other person to do as a result of your conversation? Usually, you want him to remember something, to decide something, or to take some action.

A simple step in preparing yourself and the other person is to find out whether the other person is available to talk. Simply ask, "Is this a good time to talk?" or, "Do you have 10 minutes to talk?" If the other person says no, then schedule a time to talk. This is especially important before initiating a conversation with a person with a Direct or Systematic style, but less so with a Considerate. And a Spirited person is always ready to talk!

Another aspect of preparing yourself and the other person is determining what assumptions you and the other person have. Assumptions are the result of our upbringing, life experiences, and current circumstances. Sometimes they are so ingrained that they become "facts." For example, if you grew up in a household where a raised voice was a sign of anger, then if someone speaks to you in a loud voice, you may assume that she is angry. On the other hand, if you grew up in a household where raising your voice was a sign not of anger but of excitement, or simply a way to be heard among many people, then if someone speaks to you in a loud voice, you may get more animated and loud yourself and not think anything of it.

The problem with assumptions is that they can be wrong, and then the conversation may get completely off track. Use the following strategies to avoid making inaccurate assumptions.

Avoid sweeping generalizations. Words such as *everyone, no one, always,* and *never* are clues that you are making sweeping generalizations.

Treat each person as the individual that he is. What is true for one person is not necessarily true for another.

Ask, for example, "When you turned down the chance to participate in the meeting, I took it to mean that you weren't interested. Is that correct?" Because people with the Direct and Spirited styles are both fast paced and action oriented, they are more prone to using assumptions as a shortcut to making decisions than are people with the Systematic and Considerate styles.

While making assumptions can mislead you and interfere with effective communication, one assumption you can make is that people have positive intentions behind their actions. If you assume that others have negative intentions, it will be difficult to have a cooperative, constructive communication. You don't have to be naïve, but acting as if the other person has good reasons for her actions is more likely to result in a productive conversation. Here's an example. Let's say you just found out that a colleague "borrowed" one of your employees to work on a project without checking with you first. Your initial reaction might be to barge into the colleague's office and accuse him: "I can't believe you took one of my employees just so you can finish your work and make my team look bad." Instead, take a more positive approach: "I'm concerned about the productivity in my department, just as you are with yours. Let's talk about how we can work together."

Send Your Message

The second step in the communication process is to send your message. The goal is to send your message clearly, and this can be accomplished in several ways. Use direct language. Often this means using "I" statements. For example, instead of saying, "Don't you think the first option was better?" say, "I think the first option was better." This is especially important for people with the Considerate style to be aware of, since their usual approach is to use indirect communication.

Another example of indirect communication that people with the Considerate style need to beware of is using hedge phrases or qualifiers. These are words or phrases that minimize your message, such as "sort of," "maybe," or "a little bit"; for example, "I was sort of thinking that it might be a good idea to extend the deadline a little bit."

Speak concisely. Share enough information, facts, and details to clarify your point, but not so much that your message gets muddled. If you have a Spirited style, you may be guilty of running on at length, and if you have a Direct style, you may be guilty of replacing facts with opinions. Speaking concisely and focusing on facts is a natural strength of people with the Systematic style.

Use repetition if the conversation gets off track. Remember your purpose, and return to that topic if the conversation has strayed. As you can imagine, people with the Spirited style might need extra help with this.

Nonverbal communication is an effective way to send a message. Picture this: a mother's arms are open, and she says to her child in a soothing voice, "Come here." Now, picture the same mother with her arms crossed, saying in a stern voice, "Come here!" They're the same words, but two different messages.

You know instinctively that a large amount of communication happens without words. Your message includes not only the words you say, but how you say them and what body language you exhibit. In order to send a clear message, you need to make sure that your verbal and nonverbal communications are consistent.[2]

Nonverbal communication includes the amount of eye contact you make, your posture (upright or relaxed, open or closed), the amount of tension in your muscles, and mannerisms or habits such as fidgeting or tapping your fingers or toes. It also includes personal space, or how close to another person you stand, and even what your workspace looks like. Another aspect of nonverbal communication is your voice: your tone of voice, rate of speech, volume, modulation, and pitch. All of these elements influence your message and how it is received.

Interpreting nonverbal communication can be tricky because people with different styles exhibit differences in how they express themselves nonverbally. For example, a Systematic person generally prefers more personal space (physical distance), while a Considerate person may interpret extra space as disinterest and take it personally. We'll look at style differences as they relate to nonverbal communication later in this chapter in the section on flexing your message.

Check for Understanding

The third step in the communication process is to check for understanding. This is something that a Considerate is likely to do naturally and throughout the conversation. Ask questions or use statements such as "Let's make sure we're on the same page." "Tell me what you've heard." "Does that make sense?" "What do you think about what I just said?" "Let's recap what we have said so far." "What questions do you have?" Your goal is to verify that the message was understood the way you intended it. If your message has not been understood or isn't clear, then you should go back and restate your purpose and your message.

Active Listening

This book has described the communication process from the point of view of the speaker. However, effective communication is a two-way conversation. Therefore, it is as important for you to develop your listening skills as it is for you to develop your speaking skills.[3] You've learned that someone with the Considerate style is usually a good listener, but this is not generally a strength of someone with the Direct style.

Active listening is more than waiting for your turn to talk. When you listen actively, you show the other person that you respect her and what she has to say. You can demonstrate this by giving the other person your full attention. Silence your cell phone, turn away from your computer, and tune out other distractions. Don't interrupt or finish the other person's thoughts. In fact, get comfortable with silence. Make eye contact, pay attention to the complete message—words, tone of voice, and body language—and respond to that. The way to respond is with paraphrasing. Reflect back to the speaker what was said, but in your own words. Paraphrasing is not simply repeating what the speaker said. Your goal is to capture the speaker's thoughts and feelings. Here are some examples:

- "You seem concerned about not being able to meet your deadlines."

- "Sounds like you're feeling overwhelmed."

- "You sound frustrated with how Mike handled the situation."

You may have noticed that paraphrasing usually involves using "you" statements, as opposed to sending a direct message using "I" statements. The good news is that if you don't exactly reflect what the speaker meant, he will explain, so you don't have to worry about being perfect—the whole point is to reach a mutual understanding.

Exercise: Practice Paraphrasing

Read each statement and think about what you could say to paraphrase.

Speaker: "He completely ignored my idea!"
Paraphrase: "Sounds like you're feeling frustrated that he's not taking you seriously."

Speaker: "That was the biggest mistake I've made since I've worked here. My boss is going to kill me."
Paraphrase: "You seem concerned about losing your job."
Or, "You sound pretty upset. Are you looking for advice about how to handle it?"

COMMUNICATION STRENGTHS OF EACH STYLE

Every style has strengths and shortcomings that influence the ability of people with that style to communicate successfully. First, we'll look at the communication strengths of each style, along with ways to round out that style to be most effective.

Direct communicators are short and to the point. You will know where you stand with a Direct person. Their conversations are likely to be focused on results, and they rarely go off on tangents.

To maximize your effectiveness as a Direct communicator, listen carefully. Don't try to tell others what they should be thinking and feeling; instead, let them tell you in their own words.

Spirited communicators are enthusiastic and persuasive. They care about their listeners and will invite you to share your opinions and ideas. They will keep things moving, so you are not likely to get bored.

As a Spirited communicator, to get the most out of your style, refrain from exaggeration or overgeneralizing. Try to stick to one issue at a time to make it easier for others to follow your train of thought.

Considerate communicators are excellent listeners. They are cooperative and easygoing, and they rarely try to manipulate others. They are usually able to see all sides of an issue and work hard to make sure that everyone is included and understood, both one on one and in group conversations and meetings.

As a Considerate communicator, to round out your communication skills, work on using more direct language and addressing sensitive or difficult issues head-on.

Systematic communicators are precise, logical, and methodical. You can be sure that their information is accurate and reliable. Their communications may be lengthy, but they will be organized. Their emotions rarely interfere with their messages.

To increase your effectiveness as a Systematic communicator, focus on more than just the facts. Understanding a message accurately involves interpreting feelings as well as facts.

COMMUNICATION SHORTCOMINGS OF EACH STYLE

Just as people with each style demonstrate particular strengths as communicators, there are inherent shortcomings associated with each style that can undermine effective communication. In this section, you'll see highlighted one behavior that may be difficult for people with a particular style to perform well, yet that is still an important element of effective communication. The bottom line is that everyone needs to do all of these things well.

Direct. Be direct without being rude. Direct people sometimes forget to use tact when communicating. Tact and diplomacy build rapport with others, especially with people with the Considerate and Spirited styles, and that in turn improves communication. Remember, honesty is not the same thing as tact, so saying, "I was just being honest" does not let you off the hook. Think about being authentic yet sincere. Here are some examples:

Tactless: "That's the dumbest idea I ever heard."

Tactful: "I'm having a difficult time seeing how that will solve the problem."

Tactless: "You're not going to do that, are you?"

Tactful: "I'd like to understand your reasons for doing that."

Tactless: "Don't screw this up."

Tactful: "It's extremely important that we get this right. Let me know if you need any help."

Spirited. Handle criticism better. Nobody likes to be criticized, but Spirited people may respond least effectively, for example, by getting extremely defensive and perhaps even attacking the sender. Follow these tips to help you handle criticism more productively. Avoid defensive reactions—yes, this is difficult! Ask for a specific example if none has been given. Summarize or paraphrase what the other person said in order to clarify any misunderstandings. Try to look at the situation from the other person's point of view and see if that helps you understand the criticism any better. Then, assess the criticism. Decide whether it is valid and whether it is important. For example, criticism from a customer may be important, but not valid, and criticism from a coworker may be valid, but not important. Obviously, you want to act on criticism that is both valid and important, and make judgment calls on the other cases.

Considerate. Address conflict. Addressing conflict is a challenge for Considerates. They generally want to avoid it at all costs. But that isn't a productive way to handle it. (Of course, neither is insisting on getting your own way at all costs.) Considerates in particular avoid conflict because they equate it with anger, hostile feelings, and unpleasantness. Yet there are benefits from addressing conflict, especially for a Considerate: relationships are often deepened when people work through their differences.

Follow these tips to talk about a conflict productively. First, acknowledge differences in perceptions and opinions as genuine and valid. This doesn't mean that you have to agree with the other person, but it means that you understand that there are different sides to an issue that may be legitimate and worth working through. Next, separate the person from the problem. This will help depersonalize the conversation, which can help keep the negative feelings out of it. Talk about the issue and how it affects you in specific terms. For example, instead of saying, "Your carelessness is making us all look bad," you can say, "Yesterday you neglected to throw away your trash in the meeting room, and the next group had to clean it up." Finally, focus on what you both have in common, for example, "We both want our department to be recognized as having the highest standards of any in the organization." Again, this enables you to remove personal feelings from the situation, and that usually makes it easier to communicate about the conflict or problem.

Systematic. Use positive phrasing. Because systematic people are detail oriented, they often focus on what is wrong and come off as negative and critical. By learning to use positive phrasing, Systematic people can build rapport, especially with people with Spirited and Considerate styles, which will increase the effectiveness of their communication. Here's a list of typical negative phrases:

"No."

"I can't."

"I don't have time right now."

"You're wrong."

"You don't know what you're talking about."

Take a moment to think about how each of those messages could be rephrased in a more positive way. Here are our suggestions:

"Here's what I can do."

"I can . . . (describe alternative option)."

"I will have time at . . . (time)."

"Let me share the facts with you."

"Here's the information I have."

FLEXING YOUR MESSAGE FOR EACH STYLE

Following the three steps of the communication process will help ensure that your message is clear and that it is received as you intended it. However, you can speed up the process (and probably make it more enjoyable) by getting on the same wavelength as the other person. To do this, you will need to flex your style to meet the other person's preferences (see Figure 5.1). You can do this by

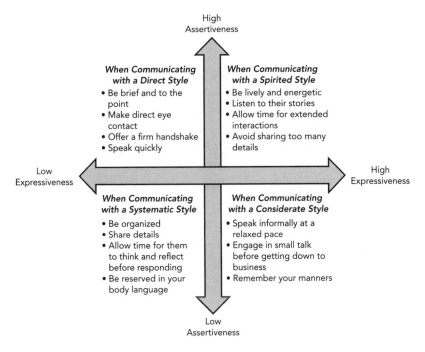

High
Assertiveness

When Communicating with a Direct Style
• Be brief and to the point
• Make direct eye contact
• Offer a firm handshake
• Speak quickly

When Communicating with a Spirited Style
• Be lively and energetic
• Listen to their stories
• Allow time for extended interactions
• Avoid sharing too many details

Low Expressiveness

High Expressiveness

When Communicating with a Systematic Style
• Be organized
• Share details
• Allow time for them to think and reflect before responding
• Be reserved in your body language

When Communicating with a Considerate Style
• Speak informally at a relaxed pace
• Engage in small talk before getting down to business
• Remember your manners

Low
Assertiveness

Figure 5.1 Flexing Your Communication Style

adjusting your nonverbal communication, as well as the focus or emphasis of your message.

Danielle and Reggie work in the alumni services department of a private university. Reggie rushed into Danielle's office and blurted, "You have to help me finish a proposal right now." Danielle responded, "I'm pretty busy right now. Can't it wait?" Reggie was insistent. "If we don't get it to the potential donor today, he's going to look for somewhere else to give his money, and I'll be in big trouble. I really need your help."

Direct Communication. Someone with a Direct style speaks quickly, speaks louder rather than softer, and usually "cuts to the chase," with little or no small talk before launching into the purpose of the conversation, so you will communicate most effectively with such a person by doing the same. Be brief and to the point. These people will make lots of direct eye contact, have a firm handshake, and may exhibit forceful or even brash body language, such as pointing. You don't have to copy their gestures, just try to match the intensity of their conversation.

In the case of Reggie and Danielle, if Danielle has a Direct style, just jumping into the topic the way he did will probably work for Reggie, although he should make it a request instead of an order, for example, "Could you help me now?" However, rather than emphasize his own dilemma, he should focus on the outcome, for example, "With your help, the university could receive $100,000 from this donor."

Spirited Communication. The Spirited person thrives on attention and recognition, so don't hesitate to call on her in a meeting or in public. Be willing to listen to her stories, and also share some of your own. Allow time for extended interactions. Keep your conversation lively and energetic. Use animated gestures, a louder voice, and lots of vocal variety. Avoid sharing too many details (unless the person asks), and don't be surprised if she tries to finish your sentences.

In the Reggie and Danielle example, if Danielle has a Spirited style, Reggie could appeal to her creativity and her desire for recognition. For example, Reggie could say, "Danielle, I could really use your help finishing this proposal. If we pull this off, it could become a model for future proposals, and it will raise your visibility throughout the donor community."

Considerate Communcation. The Considerate person wants to be your friend, so think of having informal conversations at a relaxed pace. Imagine how you would talk with a good friend, and incorporate some of those behaviors, such as lots of eye contact (though not piercing), a relaxed and open posture, and a light, cheerful voice. To work together and communicate most effectively, you want to build enough of a relationship that you can ask about something meaningful in his life—family, pets, activities, or something similar—before you get down to business. Considerates also appreciate "please" and "thank you."

In the Reggie and Danielle example, if Danielle has a Considerate style, Reggie should soften his approach to her. For example, he could begin with a simple, "How are you?" and then listen to the answer. Then he could stick with his appeal to help him out personally, since people with the Considerate style want to be supportive of others.

Systematic Communication. To communicate most effectively with someone with a Systematic style, adopt a more economical and reserved approach in your words, voice, and body language. For example, keep your voice lower and slower, and allow time for her to think before she speaks. As we've mentioned, people with the Systematic style can tend to focus more on what's going wrong with a project than on what's going right, so be prepared to address criticism in a conversation. You can skip the small talk, but realize that conversations may go on for a while because Systematics seek lots of information.

In the Reggie and Danielle example, if Danielle has a Systematic style, Reggie should change his approach so as to be less demanding and should provide more information. For example, "Danielle, I could really use your help right now. I need about 30 minutes of your time to review this proposal and make sure I haven't left out any important information."

EXERCISE: FLEX YOUR COMMUNICATION STYLE

For the following situation, decide how to flex your communication to increase its effectiveness with each style.

You have to tell someone that the proposal that he submitted was turned down.

Direct: _____

_____

Spirited: _____

_____

Considerate: _____

_____

Systematic: _____

_____

Suggested approach for each style:

> *Direct:* Get to the point immediately; be prepared for the person to dispute the case—reiterate the reasons why the proposal

was rejected, and focus on other ways in which the person can reach his goal.

Spirited: Be ready to discuss other options for getting the proposal approved; remind him of other successes he has had.

Considerate: Begin the conversation by building rapport with small talk; be clear that the rejection is related to the proposal and not the person.

Systematic: Keep your emotions in check; be prepared to answer many questions; as much as possible, provide factual details about why the proposal was rejected.

COMMUNICATING IN DIFFICULT SITUATIONS

Communication becomes much more challenging in difficult situations such as addressing a sensitive personal issue or owning up to a mistake. We don't want the other person to feel bad or get emotional, we don't want to feel bad ourselves or get into trouble, or we may be afraid we'll make the problem worse.

The first rule for communicating in difficult situations is to do it face to face whenever possible. You need to be able to use all your communication tools—words, voice, and body language—to help make sure that your message is understood the way you intended. Keep your expectations realistic—the conversation is unlikely to be easy, smooth, and stress free. However, you can minimize the negative effects by anticipating and preparing for the receiver's response (this will vary by style, and we'll look at strategies for handling each style).

Giving Constructive Feedback

First, notice that we're calling it "constructive feedback" and not "criticism." Semantics matter, and criticism has a negative connotation that will cause many people to shut down and stop listening. Constructive feedback indicates that you have positive intentions in sharing the information. You can differentiate criticism from constructive feedback in this way: criticism tells the other person what she has done wrong, while constructive feedback focuses on what she should do instead.[4] Criticism merely puts the other person on the defensive, with the temptation to attack or criticize in return. So, instead of criticizing, follow these steps.

Make specific requests, and explain your reasons. This is something that a Systematic is likely to do naturally, whereas Directs and Spiriteds may neglect the detail and explanation. Remember to focus on behaviors and actions that you want the other person to take. For example, saying, "I need you to be more of a team player," is not very effective, even if it is future-focused and not a criticism. More useful feedback would be, "I need you to participate actively in team meetings and to respond to requests from other team members within 24 hours."

Anticipate the reactions of people with each style. Not everyone is going to react the same way. Here are the potential negative reactions of each style so that you can be prepared with your response.

> *Direct:* Be prepared to stand your ground, provide specific examples, and focus on the goal for improvement. Directs may try to argue or disagree with you.

> *Spirited:* Be prepared to allow these individuals to share their feelings, then brainstorm with them for ideas on how to improve. Spirited individuals may take the feedback personally and get offended.

> *Considerate:* Be prepared to draw them out with questions and confidence-building statements. Considerates may shut down and agree with everything you say just to please you.

> *Systematic:* Be prepared by making sure you have your facts straight and organized, and allow time for them to absorb the information. Systematics may try to draw you into a lengthy discussion, refuting specific details.

Discussing a Sensitive Situation

Many sensitive situations have to do with employees' hygiene or habits. Perhaps they wear too much cologne or perfume, or they have bad breath or body odor, or they eat strong-smelling foods at their desk.

Maybe they chomp their gum or bite their nails. Perhaps they over-share personal information or continually foist their political or religious beliefs on others, belittling those who don't agree with them.

Before talking, examine your motives. Make sure your reasons for sharing this information are positive and that they support both the employee and the organization. To that end, you should be able to explain how the issue is affecting the business environment, the employee's coworkers, or even the employee's career or his potential promotions or raises. In most cases, there is a negative effect on the business environment and on relationships with coworkers and customers.

Rehearse what you will say, even practicing in front of a mirror to make sure that your words, voice, and body language are congruent. Although you will want to keep your message consistent, you can and should vary your tone of voice and body language to make the receiver receptive to your message. For example, let's say you need to tell someone that she has bad breath. Not only coworkers but also customers have mentioned it. Here are some sample statements and strategies to open the conversation in a way that is meaningful to each style. Following the opening, you want to deliver the actual information in a straightforward way.

> *Direct:* Point out the impact on her goals. "Dana, I know you want to advance in the organization, and I need to tell you about an issue that may hold you back."

> *Spirited:* Emphasize her potential. "Dana, you are talented, and you have lots to contribute to the organization. That's why I don't want this one issue to prevent you from getting the positive recognition you deserve."

> *Considerate:* Reinforce your desire to support this person. "Dana, I really enjoy working with you, and I want you to be as successful as possible. However, I need to tell you about something that is holding you back."

> *Systematic:* Take a straightforward approach and discuss the logical consequences of the issue. "Dana, I need to share some information that is uncomfortable to discuss. But dealing with it will improve your career potential."

When You Make a Mistake

No one likes to make a mistake on the job. How would you handle the following mistake?

> Mary is in charge of scheduling for a commercial painting company. As she was preparing the schedule for the coming week, she noticed that she had accidentally double-booked two large jobs. The company didn't have enough workers to cover both projects, and Mary feared that it would lose one of the clients if it couldn't meet the deadline specified in the contract.

Mistakes happen, and if you handle them proactively and professionally, they are unlikely to have any lasting adverse effects and may even enhance your reputation as a problem solver. Here are some important tips to remember.

Explain what happened, the sooner the better. People with each style have reasons for wanting to ignore it. Systematics pride themselves on their accuracy and hate making mistakes. Considerates don't like the idea of letting others down. Spiriteds don't want to be criticized, and Directs find it an obstacle that gets in the way of achieving their desired results.

However, don't assume that your mistake is too small to matter. If you project an "I don't care" attitude, that is likely to hurt your credibility more than the mistake itself. The same goes for trying to cover it up—the long-term negative impact on your reputation will be far worse than that of the mistake itself. Don't try to blame others (this is a tendency that people with the Direct style may have) or make excuses (a tendency of those with the Systematic style). Avoid exaggeration and melodrama (those with the Spirited style). Instead, focus on the realistic consequences of the mistake, and address them. Finally, don't beat yourself up for causing trouble to others (a tendency of people with the Considerate style).

Take responsibility for the mistake, and, most important, develop a plan to ensure that you don't make the same mistake again. If you can't figure out what went wrong on your own, seek input from others. People with the Systematic and Direct styles may resist asking for help; however, the feedback you get will help you become a more valuable employee. Think about how you would answer these questions: What did I learn? What will I do differently next time?

One final note: if you discover a mistake made by another person, or if you are dealing with someone who has made a mistake, don't tell him what he did wrong and what he should have done. He can't change the past. Instead, focus on what he can do in the future to make sure he doesn't make the same mistake again.

Exercise: Communicating More Effectively

Make a list of the people you communicate with most often at work. Next to each one, make your best guess as to that person's personality style and list at least one way in which you can communicate more effectively with that person (using the information from this chapter).

Name	Style	Ways to Communicate More Effectively
_____	_____	_____
_____	_____	_____
_____	_____	_____
_____	_____	_____
_____	_____	_____

▶ POINTS TO REMEMBER

- ▶ The communication process consists of three steps.

  - • Prepare yourself and the other person. Know your purpose: to inform, to persuade, or to inquire.

  - • Send your message. Use direct language, and speak concisely. Make your words, voice, and body language consistent.

  - • Check for understanding. Practice active listening. Paraphrase to reflect what was said.

▶ Style strengths and shortcomings

- *Direct*
  Strength: They stay focused and rarely go off on tangents.
  Shortcoming: They may be tactless.

- *Spirited*
  Strength: They have interesting conversations that involve the listener.
  Shortcoming: They may not handle criticism well.

- *Considerate*
  Strength: They are excellent listeners.
  Shortcoming: They may not handle conflict well.

- *Systematic*
  Strength: Their information is accurate and reliable.
  Shortcoming: They may be negative.

▶ Flex your message for each style.

- *Direct:* Be short and to the point.

- *Spirited:* Be lively and energetic.

- *Considerate:* Be friendly and relaxed.

- *Systematic:* Be factual and logical.

▶ Communicate effectively in difficult situations:

- Offer constructive feedback by making specific requests and explaining your reasons.

- When discussing sensitive situations, explain how the issue affects the employee, the employee's coworkers, and/ or the business environment.

- If you make a mistake, take responsibility for it and make a plan to make sure it doesn't happen again.

Six

MANAGING AND LEADING PEOPLE OF EVERY STRIPE AND COLOR

E very leader takes a slightly different approach to leading and managing others that is directly related to the inherent tendencies of each personality style discussed in this book.

Four MBA students are gathered at a coffee shop after class. They get into a discussion about what makes a good leader. Seth says, "Name your favorite leader." Olivia immediately responds, "One word—Oprah." Marco laughs and says, "Two words—The Donald. Donald Trump." Gabe says, "Get serious—Nelson Mandela was a great leader." Seth says, "Those are worthy choices. But my favorite leader is Bill Gates. He had the brains and the discipline to systematically outperform the competition." Olivia responds, "Oprah's leadership created fanatic followers." Marco says, "Donald Trump doesn't exactly have fanatic followers, but he's not afraid to take big risks and get big results." Finally, Gabe says, "Money isn't everything. Nelson Mandela helped reunite and reconcile former enemies."

Notice the different styles that the MBA students in the coffee shop conversation mentioned. The styles range from the blunt, "tell it like it is" style of Donald Trump to the more conciliatory approach taken by a leader such as Nelson Mandela. As you will see, the most effective leaders draw on their natural strengths while flexing to meet individual employees' needs.

WHAT MAKES A GREAT LEADER?

So what does it take to be a great leader? Hundreds of studies and thousands of books have tried to answer that question. Some researchers and authors focus on individual traits, while others focus on situational, transformational, or servant leadership practices.[1] The debate isn't likely to be settled any time soon; however, well-rounded leaders generally exhibit four areas of focus. Great leaders

Envision the future.

Engage others.

Encourage others.

Execute results.

Every leader may be naturally drawn to one of these four elements. However, the most successful leaders usually demonstrate all four behaviors.

THE FOUR LEADERSHIP STYLES

Direct: Envision the future. Lead by taking action.

Spirited: Engage others. Lead by inspiring and motivating.

Considerate: Encourage others. Lead by supporting and developing others.

Systematic: Execute results. Lead by achieving high-quality results.

Each personality style is associated with one of the areas of focus.

Direct style leaders are primarily associated with the leadership characteristic of envisioning the future. They lead by taking action. They look for promising opportunities, seek action, and encourage risk taking and direct attention to the finish line.

Spirited style leaders often demonstrate the leadership characteristic of engaging others. They lead by inspiring and motivating. They generate excitement in others; they inspire people to think of new ideas and rally the troops to achieve a common goal.

Considerate style leaders are often associated with the leadership characteristic of encouraging others. They lead by supporting and developing others. They provide support, listen actively, and proactively ask for others' input.

Systematic style leaders often demonstrate the leadership characteristic of executing results. They lead by achieving high-quality results. They establish high standards of performance, and they direct attention toward objective data and information in order to make rational decisions.

While you probably have a natural strength in one of the four leadership behaviors, you can develop strengths in all four behaviors. Here's how.

Envision the Future

Vision is a word that is often associated with successful leaders. It can be defined as the ability to see possibilities that others don't see—and then inspiring others to share that vision. Vision is more than merely inventing cutting-edge products or figuring out how to offer innovative services. And it's more than building the biggest organization in your industry or beating your competition. Vision does not necessarily involve reacting to market conditions. It answers the question, "Who do we want to be?" It comes from within the organization, and it unites everyone involved—even customers—in a common purpose.

Here's an interesting exercise. Think of a visionary organization. Now, think of another organization in the same industry that you don't consider to be visionary. What is the difference between the two? You will probably conclude that a visionary company focuses on its own success and doesn't measure itself by what other companies are doing. Another characteristic of a visionary company is that it probably made some big mistakes along the way, but it used what it learned from those mistakes to stay flexible and open to change. Even when a visionary company has a charismatic leader (think of Apple when it was under the leadership of Steve Jobs), every employee shares the leader's passion for achieving the vision. Visionary organizations look for new opportunities and jump at them when they arise.

Think about what untapped potential exists in your department or organization. How could that translate into a vision? What opportunities might propel your organization toward that vision?

Even if you can articulate a clear vision, it's important that you involve others and gain their buy-in so that your vision inspires them to take action. In the process of envisioning the future, each style will exhibit natural areas of strength and potential limitations.

EXERCISE: WEIGHING YOUR OPTIONS

With our discussion about leadership vision and styles as a backdrop, here's a practical exercise to help you put these concepts into practice. Once you have a picture in your mind of what you want to accomplish, you need to take action to achieve that vision. That involves taking risks and making decisions. Because of the action-oriented nature of their style, Direct leaders have a natural propensity to focus on this aspect of leadership, but all styles can learn how to take calculated risks to achieve their goals.

Read the following scenario and decide what you would do:

> You are the owner of a successful car dealership. You have the opportunity to buy a dealership in a neighboring community. You will have to borrow money to purchase it, and you've never carried debt before. However, you've heard that a major chain also wants to buy it, and you're afraid that if you don't buy it and the chain does, the chain's name recognition and advertising muscle could put a dent in (so to speak) the sales at your existing dealership.

How do you decide what to do?

- Consider your options. For each option, describe the potential positive consequences of choosing that option and the potential negative consequences of not choosing that option. Systematics will be especially skilled at carrying out this step thoroughly.

- If the positive consequences of choosing the option are greater than the negative consequences of not choosing that option, then the risk is worth taking. On the flip side, if the positive consequences of choosing the option are *not* greater than the negative consequences, then the risk is not worth taking.

- Make sure you are taking (or not taking) the risk based on information and not merely on emotions. Spirited managers need to take time to be certain of their information before taking a risk ("look before you leap"), while Considerates need to overcome their fears, which may prevent them from taking a calculated risk.

- Determine your backup plan in case things don't go as planned. This will enable you to have confidence that you can handle any potential outcome.

The last piece of envisioning the future is making decisions. Which statement best describes how you make a decision?

1. "The best decisions are the result of thorough research, where several alternatives are considered, and the pros and cons of each are weighed carefully before reaching a fact-based decision."

2. "The best decisions are the result of input from a group—two heads are better than one, and three heads are better than two."

3. "The best decisions are the ones I make unilaterally. Just kidding—sort of."

4. "The best decisions are the result of brainstorming possibilities and choosing the one that everyone is most excited about."

You are familiar enough with the styles to recognize each style by those statements: (1) Systematic, (2) Considerate, (3) Direct, and (4) Spirited. Each sentiment points out the inherent strengths and shortcomings of each style as it relates to making decisions.

Direct decision makers are not afraid to take risks and want to take action independently. They may even appear to be impulsive when the logic behind their decision isn't apparent. They want to make the decisions that have the biggest potential for reward, even if they come with the biggest risks.

Spirited decision makers also like to involve others in decision making—at least in generating ideas and options. However, they can be prone to making a choice before all the information has been collected or analyzed. Their optimism about carrying out the decision successfully needs to be tempered with realism.

Considerate decision makers gather input and advice from others. They want to collaborate with others in a structured decision-making process. This approach is valuable, especially when dealing with complex decisions, but it can be a deterrent when there are conflicting viewpoints that aren't easily resolved.

Systematic decision makers are analytical and precise. They want to gather complete information and examine all their options before making a decision. They trade off speed for a careful approach and analysis. This is valuable when there is time to make a decision, but it can be a hindrance in a crisis or a time-sensitive situation.

Engage Others

The second aspect of successful leadership is engaging others.

Kelly is the manager of a team that has been experiencing lackluster performance. The organization as a whole has experienced layoffs, and while no one on Kelly's team was directly affected, morale is down. Kelly wanted to "rally the troops" and called a meeting to discuss ideas for what they could do to increase their motivation and enthusiasm. She quickly discovered that this wasn't a positive team-building activity, as individual employees disagreed mightily about what actions or activities would boost morale and be motivating. The one positive note was that no one mentioned money!

Most people would agree that the ability to motivate others is a vital aspect of leadership. While this is a natural strength of the Spirited style, all managers need to cultivate their motivation skills. Effective motivation involves taking the time to recognize an individual employee's personality style and the particular circumstances that encourage and inspire him.[2] Here are tips on how to motivate people with each personality style.

Direct employees appreciate working on new challenges and nonroutine activities. They want the power and authority to take risks and make decisions, and freedom from controls, supervision, and details. They prefer to focus on the future and on projects that produce tangible results. They want the opportunity to advance. They like to be recognized and rewarded for their "bottom-line" results.

Spirited employees thrive on recognition, praise, and popularity. They appreciate freedom from rules and regulations and would love to have other people handle the details. They want to work in a friendly and informal environment where people seek one another out for work-related discussions, as well as for general group activities and socializing. The opportunity to influence others is also motivating to Spirited employees.

Considerate employees value safety and security. They need time to adjust to change, and they prefer following practical procedures and systems. They're most confident when they're working on tasks that can be completed one at a time and have a specified area of responsibility. They like to be recognized for their dependability and loyalty and their contributions to the team.

Systematic employees value autonomy. They prefer a controlled work environment with clear expectations and no surprises. They like following routines created with careful planning. Working on specialized or technical tasks also appeals to them. They require little, if any, social interaction. They like to be recognized for achieving high standards of performance.

Here's a review of Kelly's situation. First, Kelly must realize that motivation is personal, and that what motivates one person won't necessarily motivate another. However, you can make some generalities based on personality style, and that's what Kelly should do. Read the description of each of Kelly's employees and identify the personality style of each, then read the motivational strategies and choose two that would be most effective for each employee.

> *Juan:* Juan often stops by Kelly's office wanting to shoot the breeze and talk about various projects that Kelly is working on.

> *Larry:* The last time Larry worked on a team project, he told his partner everything he was doing wrong and then ended up doing all his partner's work in addition to his own.

> *Christine:* Kelly is slightly miffed at Christine at the moment; she has complained about being micromanaged and treated like a rookie employee.

> *Hillary:* Hillary plans all the monthly birthday lunches and offers to help Kelly whenever she senses that Kelly is getting overwhelmed.

The motivational strategies:

- Provide lots of public praise and recognition.

- Team people up to work together on a project.

- Hand over a brand-new project to a direct report and tell him or her to run with it.

- Let him or her work autonomously, with little interference from others.

- Create a "success board" and announce each team member's performance results.

- Ask him or her to solve an unusual problem.

- Ask him or her to represent the team at an organizationwide event.

- Create a monthly brown-bag lunch gathering where employees can meet and discuss changes that are going on in the organization.

Here are the answers:

Juan. Personality style: Spirited. Provide lots of public praise and recognition; ask him to represent the team at an organizationwide event.

Larry. Personality style: Systematic. Let him work autonomously, with little interference from others; ask him to solve an unusual problem.

Christine. Personality style: Direct. Hand over a brand new project and tell her to run with it; create a "success board" and announce each team member's performance results.

Hillary. Personality style: Considerate. Team her up to work together with others on a project; create a monthly brown-bag lunch gathering where employees can meet and discuss changes that are going on in the organization.

Encourage Others

Effective leaders support and develop their employees—in other words, they act as coaches. A foundation of effective coaching is building trust and increasing rapport, which are natural strengths of the Considerate style. While coaching may be easiest for Considerate leaders, people with all styles can be effective coaches.

Once again, while it's important that you recognize your own style's strengths and potential shortcomings, even more benefits come from flexing to your employees' styles. Let's look at how to adjust your approach to best meet the preferences of each style.

THREE-PART COACHING MODEL

Follow this simple three-part coaching model to help an employee improve her performance.

1. *Analyze.* Assess the employee's current situation: skills, abilities, job knowledge, and other such information. Identify any gaps between the employee's current performance and the desired results. Typically, you will base your assessment on firsthand observations and talking with the employee. You may also solicit input from the employee's coworkers and/ or customers. Managers with a Systematic style will naturally gravitate toward this step, while those with a Considerate style may be hard-pressed to focus on shortcomings or on situations that they may see as potential areas of conflict with the employee.

2. *Offer feedback.* Be respectful. Coaching involves two-way communication; it isn't just you telling the employee what to do! Focus on the future—the employee can't change his past behaviors; he can change only his future behaviors. Point out gaps between the current and desired performance, and also highlight positive behaviors and performance.

   Make certain your comments have the characteristics of effective feedback:[3]

   - *Timely.* The closer in time the feedback occurs relative to the behavior you want to support or change, the more influence you have to reinforce or redirect that behavior.

   - *Specific.* Feedback should address observable behaviors and actual performance rather than bad attitudes or intentions based on assumptions. For example, say, "You were late twice last week," rather than, "You're lazy."

   - *Relevant.* Feedback should relate to agreed-upon standards and performance goals. For example, if it doesn't matter when the employee comes in to work, then don't comment on her arrival time.

- *Balanced.* Feedback shouldn't be just negative. In fact, research has found that a ratio of at least 3:1 positive to negative interactions results in more productive teams than situations in which the ratio of positive to negative feedback is below that.[4]

  Direct managers will not hesitate to offer feedback, but they need to be careful not to sound too harsh. Considerate managers will lavish positive feedback on their employees and need to make sure that they don't neglect negative feedback. Spirited managers may need to work on being timely and specific when they offer feedback, while Systematic managers will have no trouble being specific but may need to work on offering balanced feedback.

3. *Develop an action plan.* Define your objectives, describe the situation, and gain agreement on the facts with the employee. Depending on the employee's style, you may brainstorm and discuss options, or present a suggested course of action. Confirm the plan in writing, set deadlines to follow up, and then follow up.

Direct. When coaching a Direct employee, be prepared and stick to business. Keep the session moving and communicate quickly. Do offer positive feedback, but you can be straightforward when giving negative feedback without worrying about hurting the person's feelings. When it comes to developing an action plan, give him alternatives so that he feels that he is in the driver's seat making decisions about his future. Don't be wishy-washy; don't speak hesitantly or too slowly; don't make decisions for him or give him work that he perceives as nonchallenging.

Spirited. When coaching a Spirited employee, be energetic and enthusiastic. Allow her to provide input and ideas. Be aware that her natural optimism may mask a lack of specifics about how to improve her performance. If you need to give this employee negative feedback about her work, separate the person from the performance so that she doesn't feel rejected personally. When developing an action plan, brainstorm with the employee, but be sure to put the ideas and suggestions in writing for follow-up, and attach deadlines. This will help the Spirited employee remain on track. Ineffective actions with a Spirited employee include being formal or impersonal, speaking too slowly, and talking down to her.

Considerate. When coaching a Considerate employee, bring lots of patience. Show a sincere interest in the employee as a person, and allow time to build rapport. Encourage him to open up and share what he's thinking and feeling. Allow silence—give him time to respond to your suggestions, for example; avoid becoming uncomfortable with the silence and putting words in his mouth. When offering feedback about a big change, break it down into smaller, easy-to-implement actions, rather than presenting it as one overwhelming change. When developing an action plan, Considerate employees will benefit from a suggested course of action that includes helping them prioritize their work. Follow up on a regular basis to see if they have any questions or concerns.

Systematic. When coaching a Systematic employee, be prepared with facts and data to support your comments and suggestions. Your opinion won't be enough to sway her. Create a specific action plan that focuses on the quantitative results and the quality expected. Actions to avoid are offering feedback without facts to back it up, getting too personal, and using a loud voice and big gestures.

The purpose of coaching is to improve performance, so the best measure of whether or not your coaching was successful is if it resulted in a positive change in behavior.

EXERCISE: FLEXING YOUR COACHING STYLE

Read the following scenario and think about how you would adjust your approach to offer the most effective coaching to people with each style.

Liz has run into some bad luck. She has missed two important deadlines in the past month. Each time she had a reasonable explanation and promised that it wouldn't happen again. Unfortunately, the department's reputation is suffering as a result, and you're concerned that it's becoming a habit.

If Liz has a Direct style: _____

_____

If Liz has a Spirited style: _____

_____

If Liz has a Considerate style: _____

_____

If Liz has a Systematic style: _____

_____

Here are some suggestions:

If Liz has a Direct style, tell her exactly why her behavior is a problem and explain how it's affecting her reputation and results. Offer a couple of suggestions about how to prevent missing future deadlines, and ask her to commit to the one she believes would work best for her.

If Liz has a Spirited style, ask for her ideas about what to do differently, but push for a specific behavior change—not just "I'll try more."

If Liz has a Considerate style, remind her of how her behavior is affecting the rest of the group. Offer a specific suggestion for how to avoid missing deadlines in the future. Encourage her to come to you ahead of time if she foresees a problem meeting her next deadline.

If Liz has a Systematic style, provide her with specific information about how missing the deadlines has affected the results of the project. Remain calm and composed, and offer a detailed plan for how to avoid missing deadlines in the future.

Execute Results

The fourth piece of effective leadership is executing results. Vision, motivation, and coaching are pointless if the organization doesn't achieve its desired results. One key aspect of achieving the desired results is establishing performance standards. This is a natural strength of Systematic leaders; however, these guidelines will help leaders of every style be more effective.

Establish standards of performance with measurable behaviors and actions as much as possible. Standards should be written and should describe specific behaviors and actions required to execute the work. Describe performance expectations in terms of

- *Time.* Schedule, deadlines, and interim milestones.

- *Resources.* Budget, staffing, equipment, and supplies.

- *Quality.* Objective and subjective measures of success and/or satisfaction, with an acceptable margin for error.

- *Communication.* Information that is required from other sources to complete the work, expectations about project updates, and so on.

Check your standards. After you have established your standards, review them to see if they are actually practical and useful.

- *Realistic.* Standards should be attainable and focused on what is necessary to complete the project.

- *Specific.* Standards should be written so that you can assess the work in terms of "performance expectations met" or "performance expectations not met." For example, instead of saying, "strengthen relationships," say, "meet with key stakeholders weekly."

- *Measurable.* As much as possible, standards should be written so that they can be measured objectively, rather than in vague or subjective terms. For example, instead of saying, "increase employee retention," say, "increase employee retention by 5 percent in the next six months."

- *Clear and understandable.* Standards should be written in plain language that leaves no room for misunderstanding. Be sure to include the purpose of the project so that employees can connect their individual tasks to the organization's overall vision. For example, "The purpose of the new database is to increase accuracy and efficiency in reaching potential customers."

If performance is falling short, it should become evident before it turns into a crisis—if you have established interim check-in dates. When performance standards are not being met, look for the most common explanations first.

- *Unclear expectations.* Make certain that employees know what is expected of them, and that it is clearly spelled out in writing. Any expectations that you have in your mind need to be clearly communicated to the employees—Spirited managers, are you reading this?

- *Insufficient resources.* If an employee has insufficient resources to complete the work, no amount of coaching or feedback is likely to make a difference.

- *Inadequate feedback.* Some employees simply need more frequent feedback. The good news is that short, informal conversations are usually enough to keep the employee on track. Look for Considerate employees to need more feedback.

In addition to addressing these issues, if they exist, look for other factors that may improve performance and help employees achieve the desired results:

- Provide job aids or checklists to help ensure completeness and accuracy.

- Rearrange workspace and/or add more or better equipment.

- Redesign the job: simplify or eliminate parts, or change a process or sequence of tasks.

Few, if any, projects ever go exactly according to plan—especially complex projects. The ability to solve problems is critical to achieving your desired results. Let's take a look at some of the similarities and differences in how people with each style solve problems.

People with a Direct or Spirited style are intuitive problem solvers who rely on their experience and perceptions to analyze a problem. They will reach a conclusion relatively quickly, without appearing to carefully consider the problem. However, their judgment, based on past experience, is at work, allowing them to recognize issues quickly, see the big picture, and recognize the likely outcomes of each possible solution.

There are some potential pitfalls with this approach. If their instincts are off base, then their preferred solution may be incorrect or ineffective. They may have trouble enlisting support for their decision because they haven't taken the time to explain the rationale behind it. Their experience in one area doesn't necessarily translate into insights that are useful in other areas, so using their intuition isn't an effective approach in that situation. People with a Direct or Spirited style should work on following a more thoughtful and analytical approach when problem solving, especially when faced with new or complex situations, or with problems where the cost of failure is high.

Systematics are analytical problem solvers who spend lots of time examining a problem before suggesting a solution. They investigate many options, apply a logical, well-defined tool or model to analyze the problem, and select the soundest course of action. They rely on a consistent thought process to examine a problem and sort through options.

Considerates follow a similar "go slow" approach, although they are likely to spend their time soliciting input from others rather than applying a tool or model. This is valuable when the problem is complex and the consequences are far-reaching.

There are potential pitfalls with this "go-slow" approach as well. People using it may be guilty of "overengineering" solutions for problems that aren't that complex. They may take too much time to work on a problem and miss out on an opportunity that is time-sensitive.

Finally, they may suffer from "analysis paralysis"—getting stuck in the process of analyzing a problem and never recommending a solution. Systematics should work on accepting ambiguity as a fact of life in business. They can use their analytical skills to develop a quick way to prioritize issues, then make sure that they have information about the most important issues and let other (less important) issues go. That should help them make decisions more quickly. Once they see that they can trust their experience or intuition, that should give them confidence to continue to solve problems using a combination of experience and analysis.

DELEGATION AND PERSONALITY STYLES

Do you ever wish you had a magic wand that you could wave over your employees and eliminate performance problems, personal issues, petty arguments, and the like? Incorporating personality style differences into your delegation approach isn't a magic wand, but it will improve individual performance and increase employee satisfaction. People will think you're a wizard at managing others!

Delegating successfully can significantly increase a manager's effectiveness.[5] However, delegation is more than merely assigning work to others. It is transferring the responsibility—and the recognition—while maintaining ultimate accountability.

The basic steps of delegation are quite straightforward:

1. Outline the task or project—in particular, the results you are looking for and the standards by which you will measure success.

2. Delegate the outcome, not the process. Avoid micromanaging! Let employees use their creativity to figure out how to complete tasks and projects.

3. On the other hand, don't abandon them. Set firm deadlines and interim milestone dates to check in and see how the project is going.

4. Communicate to all involved so that the delegatee receives appropriate support and resources. Set expectations with the delegatee about how, and how often, to communicate with you.

5. Provide feedback during and after the process, so that the delegatee can learn from the experience and improve and do even better next time.

Let's look at delegation in the context of personality styles. What obstacles is each style likely to encounter when delegating?

EXERCISE: MATCH PERSONALITY STYLES AND DELEGATION OBSTACLES

Identify the personality style you would associate with the following statements.

1. "I'm not sure I want to delegate. I hate sounding bossy."

   Personality style: _____

   _____

2. "Delegation is a waste of time because I often have to redo the work anyway. People don't seem to care about doing a good job."

   Personality style: _____

   _____

3. "I really need to delegate because I have so much stuff going on that I can't get it all done. It just takes so much time to explain what I want."

   Personality style: _____

   _____

4. "I'd like to delegate more, but people seem to be so needy. Why can't they just follow instructions and get it?"

   Personality style: _____

   _____

Answers

1. *Considerate.* People with the Considerate style are more comfortable following orders than giving them.

2. *Systematic*. People with the Systematic style have high standards of perfection and find that others have difficulty achieving them.

3. *Spirited*. People with the Spirited style thrive on having lots of irons in the fire and would rather not spend time going over the details of a project.

4. *Direct*. People with the Direct style can be short on patience and unwilling to tolerate another person's learning curve.

Obstacles to Delegating

While everyone should follow the same basic delegation process, managers with each style face obstacles to delegating effectively.

Direct managers may have trouble delegating. They are prone to either micromanaging or wanting to do it themselves. They may come off as closed-minded, insensitive, and demanding, and they may be unrealistic in their deadlines. Because they want things done their way, they are likely to overrely on a "go-to" person whom they trust, rather than take the time to delegate tasks to someone different. If a project runs into trouble, the Direct manager may look for someone to blame.

Spirited managers may have trouble delegating effectively if they fail to focus on providing enough organization, details, and follow-through with the delegatee. They may frustrate the delegatee by giving instructions in bits and pieces over time as they think of them, and by changing their mind in mid-project about what they want and by when. They're not likely to provide much oversight, leaving open the possibility of mistakes or misunderstandings along the way.

Considerates' roadblock to delegation is their tendency to sit back and wait for instructions from others. Therefore, they may be slow to delegate to others. They may be especially reluctant to delegate difficult or unpleasant assignments, fearing that doing so may be viewed as "dumping" on others. They don't want to be seen as not doing their fair share. In the spirit of trying to be helpful, they may end up micromanaging.

Systematic managers often live by the motto, "If you want something done right, do it yourself," thus depriving themselves of opportunities to delegate. And when they do delegate, they may drive the delegatee nuts by micromanaging with what are seen as overly picky and critical standards. They may appear rigid and demotivating, since in their minds, others can never get it quite right.

It's important for you to be aware of your potential shortcomings when you delegate. Another important issue to take into account is the personality style of the employee to whom you're delegating; you should adjust your approach to suit his preferences.

Flexing Your Delegation Style

Table 6.1 summarizes some tips for delegating for each personality style.

Table 6.1 Delegation and Personality Styles

	Direct	Spirited	Considerate	Systematic
Tips for delegating effectively to each personality style	• Specify responsibility and authority • Encourage communication • Remind them to be polite	• Share the big picture • Specify the "what," not the "how" • Set specific deadlines	• Express confidence • Encourage sharing of problems and obstacles • Provide feedback	• Focus on details • Establish check-in times • Share feedback on quality of work

When delegating to someone with a *Direct* style, clearly specify the responsibility and the authority of the scope of the project. Encourage her to communicate with all involved. If something goes wrong, suggest that she avoid pointing fingers and placing blame, but instead focus the conversation on resolving the issue. Remind her to involve others and thank them for their help, even if it seems to the Direct person that the others are just doing their regular jobs.

When delegating to someone with a *Spirited* style, emphasize the big picture of what you want done. Be willing to let him accomplish it in his own way as long as you agree on the results. A person with a Spirited style is not likely to provide you with status reports, so check in

118

with him to help keep him on schedule, and make sure you establish a realistic time frame for the project (that is, build in some contingency time).

When delegating to a *Considerate*, share your confidence in her ability to complete the task or project, and offer your support along the way. Encourage her to tell you about problems and conflicts, rather than shield you from bad news. Keep an eye on the amount of work she is doing; a Considerate may put in extra work to overcome an obstacle rather than confront someone else who is causing the problem. Offer lots of positive feedback about how her help contributed to the success of the project.

When delegating to a *Systematic*, plan on focusing on the schedule, deadlines, and details. Since Systematics like to work autonomously, be sure to set up some regular check-in periods because they are not likely to come to you with updates. They don't need or expect a lot of handholding, but they will appreciate feedback on the quality of their work.

Now, apply this knowledge to the following situation:

> James is planning an offsite sales meeting scheduled for next month. His team consists of Sabrina, Jack, and Nan. Sabrina has eagerly offered her help, to the point where James is almost feeling pestered. Jack is helpful when he is asked, but he needs a lot of clarification before he feels confident about completing the task James asks of him. Nan has been basically absent from the process, dismissing it as James's baby. Holding the meeting at an offsite location was James's idea; it's the first time the company is trying it, and it took a lot of convincing on James's part to get the VP of sales to agree. Now James is overwhelmed with all the planning required, and he is almost sorry he suggested it. He has nailed down the featured speaker and breakout session leaders, but he is getting bogged down in all the logistics that meeting planning requires. He wishes he could hand the project off to someone on his team, but no one can carry it out quite the way he's picturing it, and he realizes that it's more work than one person can handle.

Analysis

1. What style does James have? What delegation obstacles is he facing based on his personality style?

   James has a Spirited style. He has lots of ideas, but little appetite for follow-through. And when it comes to planning an offsite meeting, there are many, many details to handle. He has an idea in his mind of what he wants, but he either can't or doesn't want to take the time to translate his vision into action items and tasks for his team to carry out.

2. What styles do Sabrina, Jack, and Nan have? How can James adjust his approach to delegation with each of his team members?

   Sabrina is a Considerate. She is ready and willing to help out, but she needs more direction from James if she is to be successful. James should take the time up front to explain what he wants, then schedule regular check-in times so that Sabrina feels confident about the progress she's making without bothering James all the time.

   Jack is a Systematic. He can work autonomously as long as he knows exactly what is expected of him. Again, if James takes the time to clearly set up the parameters of the project, Jack will run with it without much supervision.

   Nan is a Direct. She is uninterested in the project because she doesn't see the benefit to her. James should hand off a big chunk of the project to Nan so that she feels like she owns it, rather than making it seem like she's just doing James's work.

Micromanaging

People with each style have their own reasons for being tempted to micromanage. We alluded to some of these issues earlier. Direct managers are prone to micromanaging out of a desire to have things done exactly their way. Spirited managers may micromanage when they've let go of a project, then want to grab it back when it's not coming together the way they envisioned it. Considerates may micromanage out of a desire to be helpful, and Systematics may micromanage because they feel compelled to oversee every detail of the project. To overcome these tendencies, follow these tips:

- *Start with a question.* When you discuss a project with an employee, begin with a question, even something as simple as, "How's it going?" Then stop talking and listen!

- *State the problem, but not the solution.* Even if you think the solution is obvious, prompt the employee to share his suggestions for how to handle it. If you believe the employee's idea is deficient in some way, prompt the employee to continue thinking through the issue with further questioning. This may be particularly difficult for Direct managers, who are in a hurry and believe they know the answer, but it will pay off in the long run because the employee will develop skill and confidence that will make him a more valuable employee.

- *Watch how you say things.* Your words may be misinterpreted as micromanaging when that isn't your intention. Try saying, "Here's a suggestion … ," or, "If I were you, I'd think about … ," and end with, "but you handle it as you see fit."

EXERCISE: START, STOP, CONTINUE

Think back through the information in this chapter about leading and managing others. Get three stacks of sticky notes: red, green, and blue. Use the red sticky notes to write down behaviors and actions that you want to *stop* doing, the green for behaviors and actions that you want to *start* doing, and the blue for behaviors and actions that you want to *continue* doing in order to be a more effective manager.

▶ POINTS TO REMEMBER

- ▶ Someone with each style can be an effective leader.

  - *Direct:* Leads by taking action

  - *Spirited:* Leads by inspiring and motivating

  - *Considerate:* Leads by encouraging and coaching

  - *Systematic:* Leads by achieving high-quality results

- ▶ Effective leaders focus on four areas, each of which is a natural strength of one of the styles.

  - Envision the future: *Direct*

  - Engage others: *Spirited*

  - Encourage others: *Considerate*

  - Execute results: *Systematic*

- ▶ Each style has strengths and weaknesses when making decisions as a leader.

  - *Direct*
    Strengths: Not afraid to take risks
    Shortcomings: May jump to conclusions and act too quickly

  - *Spirited*
    Strengths: Involves others in generating ideas and options
    Shortcomings: May make a choice before enough information has been gathered

  - *Considerate*
    Strengths: Gains breadth of information through collaboration
    Shortcomings: Struggles to reach a decision when diverse opinions are involved

  - *Systematic*
    Strengths: Analytical, precise, and thorough
    Shortcomings: May get too bogged down in the details

▶ When motivating others, adjust your approach to meet the preferences of people with each style.

- *Direct:* Recognize them for their bottom-line results.

- *Spirited:* Give them praise and recognition for their ideas.

- *Considerate:* Recognize them for their loyalty and their contributions to the team and the organization.

- *Systematic:* Recognize them for achieving high standards of performance.

▶ When coaching others, flex your style to meet the preferences of each style.

- *Direct:* Be prepared and stick to business. Provide feedback in a straightforward way. Give them alternatives to choose from so that they don't feel that they are being told what to do.

- *Spirited:* Allow them to provide input and ideas. When giving negative feedback, separate the people from the performances so that they don't feel personally rejected.

- *Considerate:* Take time to build rapport, and go slowly to allow them time to open up and share their thoughts and feelings. Suggest a course of action that is broken down into manageable steps.

- *Systematic:* Stick with facts and data to support your comments and suggestions. Feedback can be candid.

▶ Take the preferences of each style into account when delegating.

- *Direct:* Focus on the scope and authority of the project.

- *Spirited:* Focus on the big picture of the project.

- *Considerate:* Focus on showing confidence and support.

- *Systematic:* Focus on schedule, deadlines, and details.

Seven

WORKING ON TEAMS

I n addition to their practical reason for existing—to accomplish specific tasks—most teams also serve as a social group or unit, the place where an individual finds a sense of belonging in an organization. Understanding how personality styles affect team functioning can improve both your performance and your satisfaction on the job.

The following example depicts a team that is not working productively.

Jeff is part of a 12-member team at a paper mill. The team is in disarray. It was given the task of improving customer care—specifically, recommending a better process for handling dissatisfied customers. The team has been working on this project for two months, and so far it has nothing to show for its work. Jeff is dismayed by the amount of gossip and the level of conflict that are occurring. Some members of the team believe that the real issue is how to decrease the number of dissatisfied customers, and that the process for handling them is secondary and is not worth addressing until the bigger problem is fixed. Other members of the team have insisted on diagramming a detailed flowchart of the current process before brainstorming new ideas. One team member declared that he had the perfect answer, and when he was ignored, he dropped out of the team and quit attending meetings. Jeff is tempted to do likewise. After all, this giant headache is on top of his regular workload.

Does Jeff's situation sound familiar? If you have been in the workplace for any length of time, it is probably easy for you to think of both a positive, productive team you have worked on and one that was inefficient and negative. If you think about it for a moment, you will probably conclude that on a productive team, everyone supported one another and worked toward a common goal, while unproductive teams were characterized by members who didn't get along or didn't care, didn't help one another, or even actively undermined one another. What do you think was the source of these differences?

Does it matter if your team is dysfunctional? Yes, it does. A study in the April 2006 issue of the *Journal of Personality and Social Psychology* found that groups of three, four, or five individuals together perform better at complex problem solving than the best of an equivalent number of single individuals.[1] Since most employees are part of a team of some kind, the fact that groups tend to make better decisions than individuals means that the potential organizational impact of functional (or dysfunctional) teams is significant.

Let's take a closer look at Jeff's team. What is the impact of personality style on team dynamics and performance? Clearly, the team is working against success. Instead of tapping into the strengths of each style, all the styles are working against each other. The group that is focused on the big ideas is probably Spirited, the group that wants to map out the current situation is probably Systematic, and the Lone Ranger who quit is probably a Direct. Jeff's aversion to conflict indicates that he is probably a Considerate.

As we've discussed, people with every style are valuable contributors in the workplace; the key is getting people with different styles to work together productively so that each collectively strengthens the whole. Here are some more specifics on each team member's style.

STYLE STRENGTHS IN A TEAM SETTING

Direct: Gets the team moving

Spirited: Infuses the team with positive energy

Considerate: Maintains team harmony

Systematic: Helps the team get things done

Direct. A Direct team member is comfortable being in charge, and often takes a leadership role. Direct team members focus on the big picture. They value decisive action, and they will push the team to take risks and engage in conflict to produce a positive outcome. They are also the team members with the most independent style.

Spirited. A Spirited team member is energetic and enthusiastic. Her positive attitude is motivating to other team members, and her constant stream of ideas gives the team lots of options and opportunities for creative problem solving.

Considerate. Considerate team members are the glue that holds the team together. Their top priorities are maintaining team harmony. They do this by being good listeners, by making efforts to get everyone involved, and by being thoughtful and caring. Considerate team members also have the most flexible style and are willing to compromise for the good of the team.

Systematic. These are the team members who get things done. These people function best when they have clearly assigned tasks with deadlines, in a culture that expects deadlines to be met. A Systematic team member values precision, accuracy, and objectivity, and the team will benefit from his critical thinking skills and attention to detail.

What makes a team positive and productive? The answer lies in how the individual team members work together. The combination of personality styles in a team influences team functioning. This might sound obvious, but it is often overlooked as a "soft" skill. An effective team works well together on two levels: tasks and relationships.[2]

1. An effective team exhibits the following task characteristics:

- Common purpose
- Clear performance goals

- Common work approach and methods

- Ability to make decisions and reach consensus

- Ability to avoid groupthink

- Accountability to the team

2. An effective team exhibits the following relationship characteristics:

- Trust

- Cooperation

- Mutual support (train and motivate one another)

- Ability to address and resolve conflict productively

Let's look at these in more detail.

THE TASK SIDE OF TEAMWORK

Whether a team is temporary or permanent, it will benefit from having the purpose and scope of the team clearly stated. Basically, the team members should be able to answer the question, "Why do we exist?"

Clear Performance Goals

- Identify the team's tasks in specific, concrete language. State the outcomes you expect from the team.

- Describe the outcomes that constitute success and the outcomes that would count as failure for the team.

- Provide a basis for deciding priorities.

Common Work Approach and Methods

This is also referred to as ground rules or norms. They may be unstated and heavily influenced by the team leader or by a Direct style team member who may exert undue influence on the team. Ground rules and norms usually relate to such things as whether or not it's important to be on time, how to make decisions (for example, by majority vote or by consensus), and how (and how often) to communicate with one another—in person, by e-mail, by voice mail, by text, as needed, weekly, daily, and so on.

Just reviewing this list, you can see that these areas will bring out the differences among the personality styles. A Considerate person will want to check in with the rest of the group frequently and is likely to want to use consensus as a decision-making approach to ensure that everyone has a say in the decision. A Spirited person may have trouble being on time and meeting deadlines and may rail against meeting schedules that she sees as too rigid. A Systematic person will probably be content with communication on an "as needed" basis, and a Direct person will probably prefer a majority vote approach to decision making. These differences need to be addressed and settled in order for a team to function at its highest potential.

Norms are beliefs and behaviors that reflect an organization's culture. They can be tricky because they're often unstated and because they sometimes contradict stated policy. They are formed by observing and conforming to behaviors that get rewarded and avoiding behaviors that get punished. Here's an example: an organization will have a stated policy about work hours; however, one organization's norm may demand long hours and face time, whereas another organization's norm may be to get the work done, and it doesn't matter where or when.

Ability to Make Decisions and Reach Consensus

An effective team uses consensus to make important decisions—but not all decisions.[3] Consensus takes a long time and a lot of work; therefore, it should be reserved for decisions that have a long-term impact on the team, affect all members of the team, and involve critical work that requires the full commitment of the team. In other situations, other forms of decision making (autocratic or democratic) are more efficient. Consensus is the process of reaching a decision that every team member fully and freely supports. In order to achieve consensus, you need to

- Include all team members in the debate.

- Promote and protect individual viewpoints.

- Treat every team member and her opinions with respect.

- On the other hand, stress the importance of individuals remaining flexible, open-minded, and nondefensive.

If you are a Considerate team member, your preference for harmony can make a positive contribution to this process. Focus on problem solving. Avoid getting attached to positions and an "I/you" or "we/they" mentality. Especially, avoid wasting time discussing issues and grievances that are unrelated to the decision at hand. If you are a Spirited team member, you can help the team by drawing on your natural enthusiasm and high energy to encourage team members to "try on" other points of view or consider alternatives. Provide a structure for debating the issues. Unstructured debate can often lead to domineering personalities taking over, which can have a negative effect on team unity. As part of the structure, provide an opportunity for someone to play devil's advocate and openly present opposing viewpoints. If you are a Systematic team member, you can fill this role well.

Prioritize the issues and map out a course of action. Summarize the differences and similarities of team members' opinions to guide the team toward a decision. If you are a Direct team member, you can serve in this role effectively.

Ability to Avoid Groupthink

When you seek consensus, make certain that you haven't inadvertently engaged in groupthink instead. Groupthink occurs when the pressure to conform outweighs a team's decision-making process. Symptoms of groupthink include rushing to quick agreement, limiting the alternatives being considered, rationalizing conflicting information, neglecting to obtain objective information from outside the group, and using "we" and "they" language. Ironically, groupthink may occur most often in high-performing teams where the pressure to continue the current level of success is high.

To avoid groupthink, develop a template to encourage objective analysis. Make a point of discussing competing points of view, seeking outside expertise to bring a fresh, objective perspective, soliciting input from team members in writing or in private, and having the team leader or the dominant team member refrain from expressing his opinion until all the others have expressed theirs.

Some personality styles are more susceptible to groupthink than others—can you guess or surmise which ones? If you thought Considerate and Direct, you're right. People with the Considerate style prefer to avoid conflict, so they are more likely to "go along to get along." People with the Direct style are often impatient and forceful and like to take quick action; therefore, they may be prone to coerce other team members to adopt their points of view.

Accountability to the Team

Make certain that responsibilities are divided equitably and that no one person is overloaded or has an unreasonable deadline. The success of a team depends on individuals being able to complete their tasks.

There are a number of reasons why plans fail or fall short:

- *Lack of well-defined tasks.* Clearly spell out the objective(s) and the deliverable(s) of each task. Every team member should know and agree on what constitutes a successful result.

- *Unclear responsibility or deadlines.* To overcome this, create a spreadsheet outlining each task, the team member who is responsible for it, and the deadline. Review this regularly (see low accountability) and revise it as necessary.

- *Low accountability.* To overcome this, use the first few minutes of every meeting to review action items from the previous meeting (or this may be done as a weekly e-mail). Ask each team member to summarize the status of any action items assigned to her. Most people will comply to avoid public embarrassment.

Review the following checklist for task-related performance as a team. Identify how each question draws on a particular style's strength as a team member.

☐ Is your team achieving or making progress toward its stated purpose? Direct team members will focus on this perspective.

☐ Are tasks clearly defined and assigned with deadlines? Systematic team members will excel at organizing this.

☐ Is information about progress and obstacles being shared? Considerate team members will emphasize this aspect.

☐ Do team members share in idea generation and decision making while avoiding groupthink? Spirited team members can lead this part of the task.

☐ Do team members feel an obligation/accountability to the team? All team members need to be accountable to the team if it is to accomplish work as a team.

THE RELATIONSHIP SIDE OF TEAMWORK

Let's switch gears and look at the relationship side of teamwork.

Trust

> You have been working on an important proposal for several weeks. Unfortunately, you have a family emergency, and you need to hand off the proposal to another member of your team for final review and presentation to senior management. Whom do you choose? Why did you choose that particular person?

Where does trust come from? It can grow through knowing someone for a long time. Or, it can be a "vibe" that you pick up immediately or without having met face to face. Sometimes, trust develops from someone's credibility and qualifications, or from firsthand knowledge of the person's performance.

There are five elements of trust: competence, reliability, intent, concern, and time.[4] *Competence* is being able to do the job you are asked to do. *Reliability* is being dependable and predictable in your behavior. *Intent* is "saying what you mean and meaning what you say." It's focusing on what's best for the team and putting your effort into accomplishing that. An important aspect of reliability and intent is not biting off more than you can chew—you may have great intentions, but if you have trouble saying no to others, and as a result over-commit and are unable to keep your agreements, others' trust in you will erode. *Concern* is having empathy and showing that you care about others. It might sound like this: "You have put so much effort into this project; it must be difficult seeing the budget cut. Is there anything I can do to help?" Finally, the last element of trust is *time*. When you have an opportunity to watch a team member's actions over time, you can decide whether the team member is trustworthy—whether her repeated behaviors demonstrate the other elements of trust: competence, reliability, good intentions, and concern.

As you think about each of the elements of trust, can you see how they hold different levels of importance for each personality style? For someone with a Direct style, trust comes primarily from competence. For a Systematic, trust comes from reliability. For a Spirited, trust comes from intention. And for a Considerate, trust comes from demonstrating concern.

How would you build trust with team members in the following situation?

Your boss has given you the task of soliciting input from the rest of the team on how she can improve. Because of this, some team members have tagged you as the boss's favorite and are reluctant to share their feelings with you. Take a moment to think about how you would approach gathering open and honest opinions from the team. Here's a rundown of your team members: Sue is a Direct, Dylan is a Considerate, Jill is a Systematic, and Scott is a Spirited.

Sue (Direct): Approach with the discussion in a frank and candid manner. Remain focused on the issue at hand and remind Sue of your experience if she questions your competence.

Dylan (Considerate): Emphasize concern. Spend time with Dylan and listen to his concerns. Use self-disclosure to build rapport.

Jill (Systematic): Focus on reliability. Review the reasons why your boss chose you to collect the input, and remind Jill of the importance of collecting information from everyone in order to give your boss a complete and objective picture of her performance.

Scott (Spirited): Focus on intention and time. Set aside a specific time for a wide-ranging discussion. Emphasize how much you value his input, and how his sharing his thoughts will influence the boss's desire to change.

Finally, let's look at trust busters; these are behaviors that you want to avoid because they will damage or destroy trust. Some behaviors are particularly damaging to specific personality styles.

- *Lying.* Lying destroys everyone's trust!

- *Not following through on commitments.* This will especially diminish trust with a Direct team member because you will appear incompetent.

- *Criticizing.* Spirited team members are particularly sensitive to criticism, and if you criticize them, their trust in you will diminish because they will question the intentions behind your remarks.

- *Shooting the messenger.* Considerate team members will feel rejected if you express your disapproval, even if it's not really meant to be directed at them.

- *Saying one thing and doing another.* Systematic team members will lose trust in you if they believe you are unpredictable because they will see you as unreliable.

Cooperation

In addition to trust, high-performing teams generally exhibit a high level of cooperation among team members. Cooperation shows up in a team's ability to make decisions and get the work done (and accomplish it without killing one another!). Cooperation can take various forms—think of how different sports teams work. The members of a cross-country team practice together and push one another to improve performance; however, their performances are timed (scored) individually, and the individual results are combined to form a team score. A football team has individual positions but must execute set plays, with team members working interdependently in order to perform effectively. And on a basketball team, every team member is involved in all aspects of play (shoot, guard, run, pass, and so on) in order to perform successfully.

Some behaviors that demonstrate cooperation are

- Exhibit collaboration rather than competition.

- Offer relevant and timely information and (solicited) advice and suggestions.

- Listen to the ideas of team members.

- Share credit for success and refrain from finger-pointing and blaming.

- Treat team members with respect; disagree with ideas without attacking people.

Mutual Support (Train and Motivate One Another)

Meaningful mutual support is more than superficial cheerleading and "attaboys." A team that offers mutual support and motivation puts actions behind its words. Instead of merely offering feel-good platitudes, team members offer to help one another in tangible ways, such as reviewing a report before it gets sent to upper management, or assisting with research to make sure that the team has all the information it needs if it is to make a good decision. Flexibility and adaptability are key to providing mutual support, and people with the Considerate and Spirited styles are especially adept at this aspect of teamwork.

Ability to Address and Resolve Conflict Productively

The diversity of personality styles on a team can lead to conflict. Since most teams are made up of a combination of personality styles, conflict is virtually inevitable. The ability to resolve conflict productively is a hallmark of an effective team. Most conflict begins as either a task-based conflict or a relationship-based conflict.[5] It's important to recognize the difference because they are resolved in different ways. However, what typically happens is that something that begins as a task-based conflict spills over into a relationship-based conflict if it isn't resolved effectively.

You can recognize a task-based conflict by such things as deadlines that are missed, tasks that slip through the cracks, or team members duplicating tasks, expressing frustration with work. and trying to find "workarounds" that will minimize their frustration but may negatively affect other team members' work.

To resolve task-based conflict, search for the root cause. Is it poor communication? A lack of knowledge or training? A poorly designed work process? The key is to focus on the "what," not the "who."

In a relationship-based conflict, style differences and incompatible behaviors are usually the source of the conflict. To resolve a relationship-based conflict, focus on meeting common goals while accepting differences in style. Seek to understand the other person's perspective, and assume positive intent—that is, assume that both sides want to resolve the conflict in a positive way.

Here are some more tips.

> *Remind yourselves of your common purpose.* This will naturally foster cooperation and get both sides back on the same page. Find the common ground, and agree on what you want to accomplish. Team members with a Direct style will naturally gravitate toward this approach.

> *Create incentives to act.* Impose a structured process to encourage action and discourage inaction. Assign deadlines and spread responsibilities among all team members. Systematics and Directs will respond to this approach.

> *Take big action using small steps.* There is often a high level of resistance in a conflict. That resistance can be overcome by taking a step-by-step approach to resolving the issue. The big action will appeal to people with a Spirited style, while the step-by-step approach works for Systematics.

> *Create small wins.* Grab the low-hanging fruit first. Tackle the easiest issues in order to gain momentum and commitment. This reinforces the feeling that successful conflict resolution

is possible. This approach will satisfy Considerate team members.

Include a few trial proposals. Use these preliminary suggestions to test options, find the weak points in a proposal, clarify assumptions, and refine priorities. Generally, teams work well when they have options to discuss, compare, and modify. Be aware that Systematics will not like dealing with half-baked ideas, whereas people with a Spirited style will use them as a jumping-off point for other, more realistic ideas. Think about the following situation:

Ginny and Tom are members of a software development team. Ginny is the veteran, having been part of the team for eight years, while Tom is relatively new, having joined the team during the past year. The team is focused on a new application that is to be rolled out next month. Some features and functions are missing or are not working as envisioned, and Ginny and Tom are arguing about how to fix these issues before the rollout. Ginny believes that they need to hold a team meeting with all team members present to brainstorm ideas about what features to focus on finishing and how to get them done, while Tom believes that this would be a complete waste of time when they're under such pressure to finish. He thinks they should analyze the current bugs in the system and eliminate those before adding any additional features. Team members have taken sides and are gossiping, and the conflict has escalated to the point where the senior VP has heard about it and has demanded a meeting with Ginny and Tom.

Analysis

1. Is this a task-based or a relationship-based conflict?

2. What personality styles are involved?

3. If you were Ginny, what strategies would you use to resolve the conflict?

4. If you were Tom, what strategies would you use to resolve the conflict?

Suggestions

1. Is this a task-based or a relationship-based conflict? In other words, where should problem solving begin?

   This began as a task-based conflict—the work is not getting done on time; however, it has clearly developed into a relationship-based conflict. The intensity of that aspect of the conflict should be addressed first, or de-escalated, allowing the team members to look at the "what" of the problem.

2. What personality styles are involved?

   Ginny, with her focus on ideas and brainstorming, reflects a Spirited style, whereas Tom, with his focus on analyzing, reflects a Systematic style.

3. If you were Ginny, what strategies would you use to resolve the conflict?

   Ginny can help resolve the conflict most effectively by flexing to Tom's Systematic style. Therefore, she should try creating a structured approach to problem solving, perhaps by setting short-term deadlines for brainstorming sessions, and after identifying big goals to work toward (for her), breaking those goals into smaller steps that can be implemented incrementally (for Tom).

4. If you were Tom, what strategies would you use to resolve the conflict?

   Tom can help resolve the conflict most effectively by flexing to Ginny's Spirited style. Therefore, he should try focusing on their common goal, and identifying a big idea (for her) that can be broken down into smaller steps (for him).

ALL ABOUT TEAM ROLES

Does the following scenario sound familiar?

Imagine this: You are a brand new team member in the actuarial department of a large insurance company. As you sit down to attend your first team meeting, you're naturally curious about everyone, and you notice everything that is going on. Here's what you see: one team member is talking nonstop to another, who is nodding her head vigorously in response to everything the speaker is saying. The speaker is Troy, the "superstar" of the team according to pretty much everyone, and the other person is Catherine, who has a reputation for taking on a lot of the "drudge work" for Troy, enabling him to maintain his superstar status. Also present is Carlos. You've heard that he is a steady and reliable worker, even if he seldom offers the most innovative ideas. Finally, there's Penny, who's a bit of a wild card, according to your boss—sometimes she's inspiring and encouraging, and other times she gets so wrapped up in her own ideas that she can zap the productivity of the team.

As the meeting begins, Troy takes control. He is impatient and critical of the presentation that Penny is giving because she is trying to involve everyone else, and Troy is in a hurry. Penny immediately shuts down, and Carlos shoots dirty looks at Troy and tries to make Penny feel better. Catherine is busy scribbling notes and doesn't look up much. It looks as if it's going to be another long meeting dominated by one person where not much gets done.

People are hired on an individual basis to fill specific positions and take on specific tasks and responsibilities on behalf of the organization. Once these people are put into teams, they take on roles and responsibilities as team members that are usually unrelated to their primary positions, but that nevertheless play an important part in how well the team and the organization perform.[6] Personality style preferences affect what roles team members are naturally drawn to. However, the shortcomings of the various personality styles are reflected when negative team roles are present. While team members may naturally fall into roles that draw on the strengths of their personality style, it is wise to consciously assign team roles to specific team members in order to maximize personality style strengths and minimize trouble spots.

Think back on the scenario presented. Can you identify the personality style of each team member? What positive and/or negative characteristics did each team member exhibit?

Troy demonstrated a Direct style with his assertive approach. He took a leadership role in the meeting, but he also displayed a negative characteristic by being harshly critical of Penny.

Penny exhibited a Spirited style when she involved everyone in her presentation (and also based on the boss's assessment of her as both inspiring and distracting). She was a positive contributor in trying to involve everyone, but perhaps she backed down too quickly when Troy criticized her approach.

Carlos clearly showed a Considerate style in this situation when he tried to make Penny feel better (as well as based on his description of being a steady helper). He appeared to be mainly focused on maintaining harmony among the group.

Catherine's style was Systematic, based on her appearing to take careful notes during the meeting and handling much of Troy's detailed, nitty-gritty work. Catherine is probably a valuable worker who gets things done.

Productive Team Member Roles

These are the responsibilities that will enable a team to function well—to make good decisions in a timely manner and carry out its work with a minimum of misunderstanding and conflict.

- *Initiator.* Gets important discussion going; great at brainstorming.

- *Implementer.* Follows through once decisions have been made.

- *Investigator.* Gathers information and data.

- *Communicator.* Keeps everyone in the loop.

- *Organizer.* Assigns roles and responsibilities.

- *Encourager.* Maintains motivation and enthusiasm among team members.

- *Harmonizer.* Maintains harmony and minimizes conflict among team members.

- *Evaluator.* Monitors progress and determines accomplishment.

Let's review the strengths of each style in a team environment.

Direct. Someone with this style focuses on the big picture, communicates quickly and concisely, and is willing to take risks, ask tough questions, and raise difficult issues.

Spirited. Someone with this style exudes energy and enthusiasm, loves to brainstorm and generate new ideas, is open to change, recognizes and praises the input and suggestions of others, and enjoys socializing before getting down to business.

Considerate. Someone with this style listens carefully, encourages everyone to share ideas and feelings, is willing to jump in and help out when needed, mediates conflict and maintains harmony within the team, and demonstrates supportive body language—lots of eye contact, head nodding, and other such actions.

Systematic. Someone with this style has strong organizational skills, pays attention to detail, thinks critically and analytically, has high standards of performance, and focuses on business issues before socializing.

EXERCISE: MATCHING PERSONALITY STYLES AND PRODUCTIVE TEAM ROLES

Using the information you just learned, match each productive team role with the style that most naturally supports that role.

Productive Team Role	Ideal Style
Initiator	
Implementer	
Investigator	
Communicator	
Organizer	
Encourager	

Productive Team Role	Ideal Style
Harmonizer	_____
Evaluator	_____

Answers:

Productive Team Role	Ideal Style
Initiator	Spirited
Implementer	Systematic
Investigator	Systematic
Communicator	Considerate
Organizer	Direct
Encourager	Spirited
Harmonizer	Considerate
Evaluator	Direct

Shortcomings of Each Style in a Team Environment

Any strength that is overused becomes a limitation. It's important to be aware of what happens when people with each style become stressed or encounter pressure that causes the individual to overrely on her preferred behaviors until she becomes detrimental to and undesirable in the situation.

- *Direct.* Can become impatient, overly critical, and insensitive to the receiver's feelings when giving negative feedback.

- *Spirited.* Can become undisciplined and distracted, have difficulty sticking to the plan, struggle to meet deadlines, and perceive rejection where it was not intended.

- *Considerate.* Can become passive, dependent, too trusting, reluctant to express opinions, and overly sensitive to criticism.

- *Systematic.* Can become rigid, inflexible, resistant to change, and a perfectionist, and values data over relationships.

Unproductive Team Member Roles

Likewise, negative team roles can develop when individual team members, or the entire team, are stressed or under pressure. Here's a description of some of those behaviors:

- *Naysayer.* Is never satisfied; focuses on the problems.
- *Procrastinator.* Has difficulty meeting deadlines.
- *Dominator.* Wants his opinions to be heard loud and clear.
- *Know-it-all.* Wants to show off her knowledge and expertise.
- *Wallflower.* Doesn't feel secure sharing his opinions.
- *Judger.* Jumps to conclusions.
- *Yes person.* Goes along with everything; is reluctant to exhibit independent thinking
- *Nitpicker.* Finds fault with imprecise information; splits hairs over data.

EXERCISE: MATCHING PERSONALITY STYLES AND UNPRODUCTIVE TEAM ROLES

Again using the information you just learned, match each unproductive team role with the style that is most likely to exhibit that tendency when under stress or facing pressure.

Unproductive Team Roles	Style with This Tendency
Naysayer	_____
Procrastinator	_____
Dominator	_____
Know-it-all	_____
Wallflower	_____

Unproductive Team Roles	Style with This Tendency
Judger	_____
Yes person	_____
Nitpicker	_____

Answers:

Unproductive Team Roles	Style with This Tendency
Naysayer	Systematic
Procrastinator	Spirited
Dominator	Direct
Know-it-all	Spirited
Wallflower	Considerate
Judger	Direct
Yes person	Considerate
Nitpicker	Systematic

Virtual Teams

Virtual teams are becoming more and more prevalent in the workplace. They offer benefits to both the organization and the employees. They save organizations money by reducing necessary office space, and organizations can recruit and hire employees with special skills who are not located near the office and wouldn't be willing to move. They can also combine employees from separate offices to create a team with special expertise. In addition, most employees report an increase in productivity when they work virtually,[7] as well as a reduction in stress from eliminating commuting and enhancing the ability to juggle multiple priorities.

The IDC (International Data Corporation) estimates that by 2013, 75 percent of the American workforce and 35 percent of the global workforce will be mobile. A 2008 survey conducted by World at Work found that 17.2 million Americans are telecommuting, a 70 percent increase from 2005.[8]

In many respects, virtual teams operate the same way as regular co-located teams do. And just as in regular teams, the strengths and shortcomings of each personality style will be apparent.

Benjamin, Chris, Steve, and Angela are a virtual team holding a regular team meeting via a conference call. Benjamin kicks off the call by asking how everyone is. Chris changes the subject and asks if everyone has the agenda. Steve excitedly jumps in and starts talking about a topic in the middle of the agenda, and Angela says nothing.

What is each team member's preferred style? And how can they support one other so that they are as productive as possible in a virtual team environment?

Benjamin: Considerate

Chris: Direct

Steve: Spirited

Angela: Systematic

Here's a description of how people with each style are likely to behave in a virtual team, as well as tips for how to draw out the best performance from each style.

Directs' candid and perhaps outspoken approaches can come across as brusque or even rude, especially in a virtual environment, as all communication occurs through words and important body language cues are missing. They will not be interested in including small talk in the meetings, and they will want meetings to be to the point. To make the most of a Direct in a virtual team environment, try to keep the pace moving. Be prepared and review all materials and issues to be covered before the meeting begins. Be succinct in your comments, and stay on point. Table any unrelated topics that may come up during the discussion.

Spirited team members thrive on energy and enthusiasm from others, and will miss that in a virtual environment. They will want to spend meeting time tossing around ideas and discussing a wide range of topics. To bring out the best in a Spirited team member, allow some flexibility or wiggle room in the agenda in case you get off topic. Consider scheduling special brainstorming sessions, and be sure to show your appreciation for him and recognize his accomplishments during your meeting time.

Considerates, although expressive, are likely to be quiet during virtual meetings, preferring to wait and hear everyone else's opinions and input before sharing their own. Since they enjoy interacting with team members, they may not automatically thrive in a virtual team. So, to make the most of a Considerate in a virtual team environment, either begin each meeting with time for small talk or make an effort to contact the Considerate person outside of the meeting time to connect on a more personal level. Ask questions directly to Considerate team members to draw them out.

Systematics are detail oriented and can be relied upon to complete their work accurately and precisely without oversight. To bring out the best of a Systematic in a virtual team environment, be patient. Allow plenty of time to share details, and get comfortable with silence while Systematics process and analyze what they've heard.

EXERCISE: IMAGINE THE FUTURE

Imagine that it is one year from today, and your team is performing more successfully than ever. What are you doing differently from what you are doing today, as an individual and as a team? How are you working together differently on tasks? How are you interacting differently in your relationships? How are you handling conflict? And how did you and your team get from where you are today to what you're imagining in the future?

_____

_____

_____

_____

_____

_____

_____

_____

▶ **POINTS TO REMEMBER**

- ▶ People with each style offer strengths as team members.

  - *Direct:* Leads the team to action

  - *Spirited:* Motivates the team

  - *Considerate:* Maintains team harmony

  - *Systematic:* Organizes the team's activities

- ▶ High-performing teams accomplish tasks by using strategies that appeal to each personality style.

  - Share a common purpose: Direct

  - Identify a common work approach and methods: Spirited

  - Make decisions together: Considerate

  - Set clear performance goals: Systematic

  - Establish accountability to the team: all

- ▶ High-performing teams use consensus to make important decisions, and they draw on the strengths of each style to reach consensus.

  - Prioritize the issues and map out a course of action: Direct

  - Focus on problem solving: Spirited

  - Include all team members in the debate: Considerate

  - Provide a structure for debating the issues: Systematic

- ▶ Successful teams build trust by addressing each personality style's need for trust.

  - Competence: Direct

  - Intent: Spirited

  - Concern: Considerate

  - Reliability: Systematic

  - Time: all

▶ High-performing teams call on people with each personality style in order to resolve conflicts productively.

- Remind you of your common purpose: Direct

- Include trial proposals: Spirited

- Create small wins: Considerate

- Create incentives to act: Systematic

▶ Consciously assigning positive team roles to people with specific styles improves the productivity of the team.

- *Direct:* Organizer and Evaluator

- *Spirited:* Initiator and Encourager

- *Considerate:* Communicator and Harmonizer

- *Systematic:* Investigator and Implementer

▶ Minimize or avoid the negative roles that each style is susceptible to.

- *Direct:* Dominator and Judge

- *Spirited:* Procrastinator and Know-it-all

- *Considerate:* Wallflower and Yes person

- *Systematic:* Naysayer and Nitpicker

Eight

You Can
Get Along with
Your Boss

The boss's style of management directly influences the attitudes of employees who work under him.

Philip has been a midlevel manager at a construction company for 10 years. He and his former boss, Keith, had a great relationship during those years, and he really enjoyed his work. He liked Keith's hands-off management style, which he described this way: "Keith basically left me alone to do my job, but gave me support when I needed it. He was great about using his influence to eliminate obstacles and make my job easier." However, for the past six months, Philip has had a new boss, Sharon. Here's what he says about her: "It was a shock when Keith left and Sharon took over. She couldn't be more different from Keith. She constantly interrupts me and adds unnecessary complication to my work. Then, to make it worse, she gets on my case for not getting it done fast enough!"

Philip's experience mirrors that of most workers. Although some people simply aren't cut out to be effective bosses, in many cases, whether you have a "good" or a "bad" boss depends solely on whether you and your boss share similar personality styles or whether your styles clash. For example, do you sometimes feel that your boss plays favorites? If so, consider this: what you see as favoritism could be an example of people with shared work styles operating on the same wavelength. It might just be that your boss finds it easier to work with a particular employee because the two of them see eye to eye on many issues.

How to Get Along with Any Boss

Clearly, the characters in the opening vignette, Philip and Sharon, are on a collision course that benefits neither of them. Philip is likely to leave (or be fired from) a job he really likes, and Sharon is likely to lose a competent and dedicated worker for her team.

The rest of this chapter shows you many ways to avoid winding up in an intractable situation like the one between Phillip and Sharon. However, before you move on, here's a simple, often repeated, but hardly ever followed truth to keep in mind:

You can't change others; you can only change yourself.

While we all might agree that this adage is true, it is still a lot easier to assign blame when you get frustrated with your boss's behavior rather than accept the situation as it is. For anything that follows to get much traction, you have to be willing to flex to your boss's style. When you change your approach, you are likely to find that your boss's response changes as well.

At the end of the day, whatever you think of your boss's style, it is your job to support him and to make your work styles compatible. For example, think about how and when your boss communicates and how your boss makes decisions. How might you adjust your work style to meet your boss's preferences? Identify the pressures, challenges, and priorities your boss has and figure out how you can help.

Put yourself in your boss's shoes and approach her actions from the point of view of positive intent. Consider that your boss probably has good reasons for behaving the way she does, even if those reasons aren't apparent to you. If you are able to see your boss in this new light, then her actions will tell you that she wants the best for the organization, for the department, and for you!

Navigating This Chapter

Now, with the right perspective in place, you are ready to begin building a better relationship with your boss. What follows is a list of every employee and boss style combination. Each combination begins with a description of a typical boss-employee interaction. This interaction highlights the similarities and differences between the two styles. Then you are offered suggested behaviors and strategies to use and not to use (all from the employee's point of view) that will guide you in developing a good working relationship with your boss. Feel free either to skip directly to the boss-employee combination that reflects your current situation or to read through the entire chapter to get a more complete picture of the possible style dynamics at work in your own organization.

Direct Boss, Direct Employee

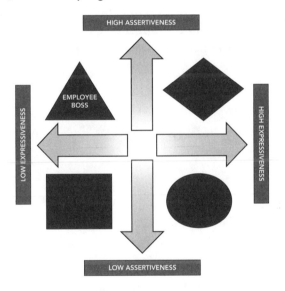

Figure 8.1 **Direct Boss, Direct Employee**

Linda works for Joe in a real estate office. Linda and Joe always seem to be knocking heads. In a recent incident, the two of them were discussing where to place a series of ads. Linda was arguing strongly for her idea: "Nobody looks at print media anymore. We'll get better results using social media." Joe retorted, "Don't be silly. We can't completely drop print ads and expect the same amount of traffic and inquiries. Just place the ads where I told you to." Linda left, shaking her head. "He doesn't listen," she thought to herself.

Behaviors to Use. Direct employees who work for Direct managers may feel that they are frequently locked in power struggles and battles for control. If you are a Direct employee working for a Direct boss, you need to accept the fact that your boss gets to direct your activities. Develop patience—this will probably be a challenge, but you like a challenge! You and your boss both like to talk, but you should make an effort to develop your own listening skills. Remember, your goal is to support your boss. Work on confronting your boss respectfully, even if your boss isn't modeling that behavior. Make sure you are focused on the same goal as your boss.

Behaviors to Avoid. Avoid talking over your boss. Don't try to go around him or do things without informing him. Your boss may appreciate your get-things-done approach, but he will not appreciate being left out of the loop.

Direct Boss, Spirited Employee

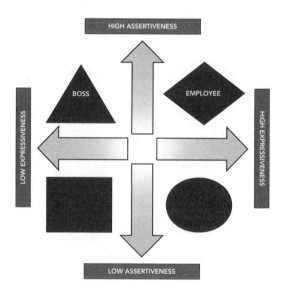

Figure 8.2 Direct Boss, Spirited Employee

Meredith supervises Brett at a local branch of a large bank. Brett sometimes feels that Meredith thinks of him as just a fun-loving employee who is not serious about his career. It is true that Brett likes to have fun at work, but he's also ambitious and wants to move ahead in the organization. He has lots of great ideas, but he has trouble getting Meredith's attention long enough to discuss them. Usually, she cuts him off quickly and tells him to put it in writing because she's too busy to talk about it at the time.

Behaviors to Use. When a Spirited employee works for a Direct manager, the Spirited employee may get her feelings hurt. If you're a Spirited employee working for a Direct manager, you need to get used to a blunt and direct style (after all, these people aren't called Direct for nothing). Adjust your style to get to the point more quickly, and consciously shorten your sentences—this may be a challenge for you! Demonstrate a greater focus on tasks and results than on ideas; again, this may be at odds with your natural instincts. You may have more success if you put your ideas in writing—highlighting the bottom-line results—than if you pitch them in a conversation.

Behaviors to Avoid. Don't take brusque or insensitive comments personally. Avoid sharing lengthy anecdotes with a Direct boss, as he will find little or no value in them. Avoid presenting too many different options at once; instead, concentrate on the results desired and focus on what is necessary to achieve them.

Direct Boss, Considerate Employee

Cathy and June work at a law firm. The two of them were co-workers until Cathy was promoted to manage all the paralegals. Now June is finding that working for Cathy is much more difficult than she expected. She knew things would be different, but she had no idea that Cathy would be so, well, bossy. June is sincerely eager to help her former colleague. But the way Cathy issues orders, it's almost as if they had never worked together and didn't know each other. There's no socializing; Cathy is always too busy to talk and is never around except to swoop in and hand out instructions. June is unsure how to improve the relationship.

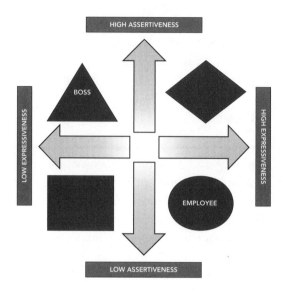

Figure 8.3 **Direct Boss, Considerate Employee**

Behaviors to Use. When Considerate employees work for Direct bosses, they may find it difficult to get on the same wavelength because they are opposite on both of the personality style dimensions. If you're a Considerate employee with a Direct boss, flex your style to match your boss's more closely by cutting out small talk and getting to the point quickly. Limit discussion and watch your time because a Direct manager tends to be more impatient than managers with other styles. These are actions that are contrary to your natural style, so it will be a stretch, but they should significantly improve your working relationship with your Direct boss. Remember to present the bottom line first, and focus on results.

Behaviors to Avoid. Don't waste time, especially on socializing. Don't take criticism personally, as Direct managers tend to be short or even terse with everyone. Along those lines, don't expect to receive "warm fuzzies" from your Direct boss. Just know that when it comes to hearing from your Direct boss, no news tends to be good news.

Direct Boss, Systematic Employee

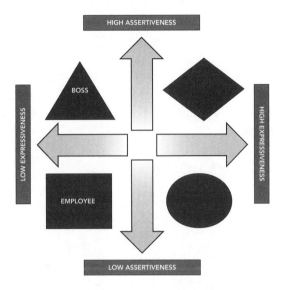

Figure 8.4 **Direct Boss, Systematic Employee**

George is a shift manager at a customer service call center. His boss, Debbie, oversees all the shift managers. George is frustrated because it seems to him that she makes rash decisions and ignores hard data if they contradict decisions that she has already reached. For example, last week he presented a proposal to change the way in which individual call center reps are scheduled. His data showed that the change could significantly decrease unplanned absenteeism. But Debbie dismissed it out of hand, saying that it wouldn't work. George is trying to figure out what it will take to convince her.

Behaviors to Use. The issues that Systematic employees face with their Direct bosses are similar to the one that George faced with Debbie. Direct bosses sometimes don't share the reasoning behind their decisions, leaving others to think those decisions are impulsive or unsound. If you are a Systematic employee working for a Direct boss, develop a "bottom-line" approach. Prioritize the information you have so that you present only the most pertinent data. This may feel uncomfortable for you, but it is a critical way to flex to your boss's style. Realize that your boss is going to make decisions differently from the way you do, that is, more quickly and unilaterally, and that she does not value data and objectivity in the same way that you do.

Behaviors to Avoid. Don't get bogged down in excessive details. Avoid taking too long to respond to your boss or to make decisions. Don't assume that you know what your boss wants; make sure you confirm any decisions with her.

Spirited Boss, Direct Employee

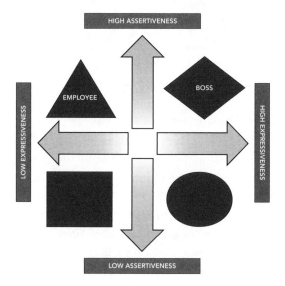

Figure 8.5 Spirited Boss, Direct Employee

Juan is a Direct employee who works for a Spirited boss, Neal, at an architecture firm. While Juan appreciates Neal's ambitious plans, he gets frustrated with the lack of follow-through. At a recent meeting, Neal was leading a discussion about whether or not to bid on a new school addition. Neal was focused on coming up with the perfect design solution, didn't feel that they had nailed it yet, and suggested that they meet again in a few days. Meanwhile, the deadline for submitting the proposal was fast approaching, and Juan thought that they should just pick a design approach and go with it, in order to make sure they met the deadline. In Juan's opinion, they could worry about tweaking the design later if their proposal were selected.

Behaviors to Use. Direct employees working for Spirited managers can be a great combination. They both like to focus on the big picture and pursue opportunities for their organization. If you are a Direct employee working for a Spirited manager, you can support your manager by being a sounding board for his ideas and by providing a reality check on what it will take to actually get those ideas implemented. You will need to develop your listening skills and patience to allow your boss to "think out loud" and sort through ideas. If your boss gives you a laundry list of projects to work on, ask him to prioritize the list so that you know what to work on first.

Behaviors to Avoid. Avoid coming across as rude or antagonistic by focusing only on the bottom line. Don't skip the small talk; Spirited managers will be more comfortable with some informal conversation first.

Spirited Boss, Spirited Employee

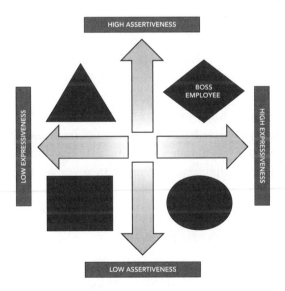

Figure 8.6 **Spirited Boss, Spirited Employee**

Tyler works for Lindsay in the marketing department of a national nonprofit organization. Tyler really enjoys working for Lindsay. They have interesting conversations, and they come up with great ideas that, if only they had enough time and money, would really propel the organization forward. The only real drawback is that Tyler has trouble completing his work. He and Lindsay will get into a discussion, and before he knows it, an hour has passed and he hasn't gotten to the work that he needs to do that day.

Behaviors to Use. Spirited employees and Spirited managers are two peas in a pod when it comes to what they think is fun at work—shooting the breeze, brainstorming ideas, and thinking big. Since the employee's job is to support her manager, Spirited employees need to become more detailed and focused on implementation, even if this is less fun and/or more difficult. If you are a Spirited employee working for a Spirited manager, you should support your manager's free thinking and desire to keep all options open up to a point, but then you need to help your manager close out the discussion and make a firm decision. You can help your Spirited manager get more organized using creative visual cues and tools, such as brightly colored floral folders instead of "plain vanilla" manila folders.

Behaviors to Avoid. As a Spirited employee, you should avoid letting spontaneous discussions with your Spirited manager override important tasks that must be completed. You should avoid becoming distracted by your Spirited boss's lack of organization. Although Spirited managers may be content to leave the details to be figured out later, going along with this approach can backfire when the time comes to carry out the plan or decision. Instead, follow up with your understanding of what was discussed to make sure it aligns with your manager's vision.

Spirited Boss, Considerate Employee

Robert is the director of sales for a women's apparel business. Julia has worked as Robert's assistant for two years. Everyone

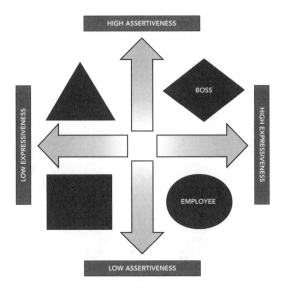

Figure 8.7 **Spirited Boss, Considerate Employee**

knows that if you need something from Robert, the fastest way to get it is to go through Julia. Robert relies on Julia to keep him organized, keep his schedule, and just generally keep track of his life. Julia likes working for Robert, but sometimes his exuberance and his whirlwind pace wear her out. She can tire of his constant last-minute changes of plans, which he finds stimulating, but which simply create more work for her.

Behaviors to Use. Considerate employees don't have the same fast-paced energy as their Spirited bosses. If you're a Considerate employee working for a Spirited boss, speed up your natural pace and move through decisions and actions at a rate that may feel uncomfortable to you. Work on increasing your own energy to match your boss's. Your natural listening skills will serve you well, as your Spirited manager likes to talk! To meet your need for positive reinforcement, ask for informal verbal feedback about how you're doing. Though it may be difficult for you, speak up when something is bothering you—your Spirited boss will probably be more than willing to find a solution that meets your needs.

Behaviors to Avoid. Avoid staying at your comfortable, slow pace. Don't spend too much time listening and not talking; your Spirited manager values employees who contribute ideas and positive energy to the group. Avoid asking for constant feedback, as this can make you appear needy.

Spirited Boss, Systematic Employee

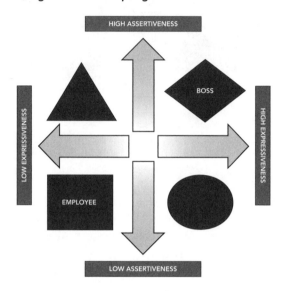

Figure 8.8 **Spirited Boss, Systematic Employee**

Dana is the owner of an art gallery. In addition, she manages a separate gathering space where she organizes exhibitions, poetry readings, and musical events; she also rents out the space to other groups. Dana recently hired Tricia to help her out with several major projects—she wants to renovate the space, add new artists to her gallery, and plan a traveling exhibit. Tricia doesn't know where to start because every day Dana tells her something different to do. Dana has papers scattered everywhere, but when Tricia tried to organize and file them, Dana freaked out. She's never had anyone work for her before, and she is having trouble letting go of control, especially to someone who has definite ideas about how to organize Dana's workspace and systems.

Behaviors to Use. If you're a Systematic employee working for a Spirited boss, you need to be ready to change gears frequently. This will feel especially uncomfortable to most Systematic employees. Emphasize to your boss how getting organized will free up more time for all his various projects and activities. Make sure your manager feels that you have helped him explore all the options or alternatives at hand. Allow time for spontaneous interactions and personal sharing; again, while this may feel like unproductive time to you, it goes a long way toward building a trusting relationship that will result in your Spirited manager giving you the autonomy you desire.

Behaviors to Avoid. Avoid appearing inflexible. Beware of shutting down discussions too soon. Avoid relying on data alone to persuade your boss of your point of view; you must also show how your ideas affect people and alliances across the organization.

Considerate Boss, Direct Employee

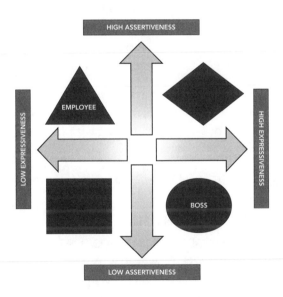

Figure 8.9 Considerate Boss, Direct Employee

Jerome works for Ashton at a social services agency. Ashton loves her job and loves knowing that she is helping people in need. She treats her employees like family and frequently checks in with them to make sure they are feeling cared for. All of this feels a bit "touchy-feely" to Jerome. A recent meeting is a perfect example: Ashton gathered her group together to develop a new process for handling client meetings. To Jerome, the solution was immediately obvious, and he felt that it was a waste of time to go around the room to hear everyone's ideas.

Behaviors to Use. Considerate managers are often easy to work for. They're easygoing and sociable, and they seek compromise in contentious situations. However, tension can arise between Direct employees and Considerate managers as a result of their being on the opposite ends of the personality style dimensions. For example, as a Direct employee, you may get frustrated with your Considerate manager's laid-back style, which is in direct contrast to your action-oriented style. And you may see her willingness to compromise as a weakness. Remember, it is your role to flex to your boss's style, so you need to develop a friendlier, more relaxed approach. Allow more time for interactions with your boss, demonstrate empathy, and be willing to make compromises to help support your boss's goals.

Behaviors to Avoid. Avoid making remarks that may be interpreted as personal criticism. Avoid taking a forceful approach that may put off your Considerate boss. Avoid behaving with indifference.

Considerate Boss, Spirited Employee

Sofia works for Jamal at a children's museum. The museum is in the midst of expanding its programming, and Jamal feels overwhelmed. Sofia has lots of ideas that would help him out, and Jamal seems to appreciate hearing them, but he hasn't tried any of them. For example, Sofia has offered to take on additional responsibilities to alleviate Jamal's workload. To Sofia, having some different tasks to work on would make her job more interesting. However, Jamal has hesitated, concerned

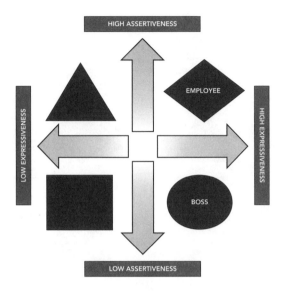

Figure 8.10 **Considerate Boss, Spirited Employee**

that Sofia already has enough to do and he doesn't want to overburden her.

Behaviors to Use. Spirited employees can sometimes overwhelm their Considerate bosses with their whirlwind approach to tackling work. While they share space on the Expressiveness dimension, they are apart on the Assertiveness dimension, which can cause tension and create stress when it comes to working together. If you are a Spirited employee working for a Considerate manager, slow down your natural pace and stick to focusing on what your boss is focused on. Give your boss your full attention, and show confidence in his decisions. Remember that an important aspect of your job is to help your boss achieve his goals; therefore, stretch your style and work on improving your skills at following up on projects and details.

Behaviors to Avoid. Some behaviors will weaken your working relationship with your Considerate boss. Don't make your boss feel rushed, and don't count on spur-of-the-moment discussions to meet your boss's need to feel that everyone has been included in planning and decisions.

Considerate Boss, Considerate Employee

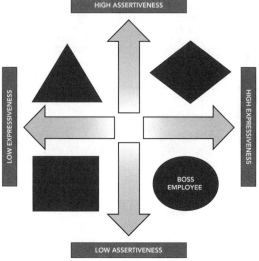

Figure 8.11 Considerate Boss, Considerate Employee

Listen to Mark describe his boss, Miguel: "His support and personal attention was unbelievable. I know he drives other departments crazy with his meddling, but I think he is looking at everything that needs to be done and is trying to help. I don't know why others don't see it that way." Mark went on to say, "Miguel will always stick up for me. I want to show him that same loyalty, so sometimes I hesitate to speak up when I disagree with him. For example, last week we were discussing a potential shipping problem. I thought we should get in touch with our customers ahead of time, but Miguel thought we should wait and see if it turns out to be a problem. I could see his side, so I didn't say anything, even though I thought my approach was better."

Behaviors to Use. Obviously, Considerate employees and Considerate bosses have much in common. That can work well and can make it easy for a Considerate employee to support a Considerate boss. For example, a Considerate employee's excellent listening skills will make her boss feel supported. However, when the employee and the boss share a style, sometimes the employee needs to make an effort to compensate for the shortcomings of their mutual style. For example, as a Considerate employee, you may need to address conflict in a way that feels more pushy to you than you'd like.

Behaviors to Avoid. Avoid being overly sensitive to your boss's feelings if it prevents you from expressing a need you have or if it impedes getting important work done. Avoid burying conflict, as it might create resentment in the long run.

Considerate Boss, Systematic Employee

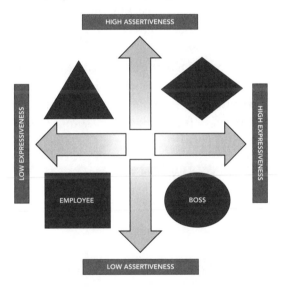

Figure 8.12 **Considerate Boss, Systematic Employee**

Carly is Terrell's boss; they work at the headquarters of a frozen food business. Terrell is concentrating on finishing a proposal for developing a new line of products. Yesterday, Carly stopped by Terrell's desk a number of times to ask about the proposal. Carly's questions were an intrusion to Terrell; he perceived them as an indirect criticism of his ability to complete the proposal. He tried to be polite to Carly, but what he really wanted was for her to leave him alone to work on the proposal. In his mind, they had already discussed it enough, and she should trust him to do his usual accurate and thorough work.

Behaviors to Use. Systematic employees and Considerate bosses are both on the low end of the Assertiveness dimension, so their work styles are likely to be similar in that they both prefer a thoughtful, deliberate pace. However, they differ in Expressiveness, and that may become evident, as Systematic employees generally prefer to work alone, while their Considerate managers want to include everyone. This can result in the Systematic employees feeling smothered. If you are a Systematic employee working for a Considerate boss, realize that what you perceive as interference most likely stems from your boss's desire to support you. Therefore, take the time to share your feelings and concerns with your boss—while this isn't your cup of tea, it may actually help your boss feel involved enough to back off and allow you to work autonomously.

Behaviors to Avoid. Avoid insisting on complete independence; while this is a good quality to have in an employee, Considerate bosses seek more involvement in their employees' work, or at least need you to give them more frequent feedback on how things are going.

Systematic Boss, Direct Employee

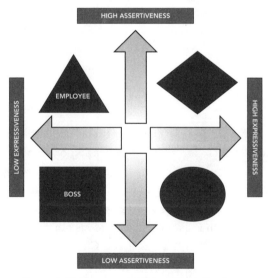

Figure 8.13 **Systematic Boss, Direct Employee**

Bruce is the manager of technical services for a large cable company. Jayden has worked for him for six months. Jayden appreciates Bruce's detailed oversight when it comes to the quality of their company's products and services, but she feels micromanaged when it comes to getting her own work done. "I feel like Bruce is always looking over my shoulder, and that bugs me. I know what I'm doing, and if he would just leave me alone to do my job, I'd get a lot more done." Of course, Bruce believes he is being a good manager precisely because of the close attention he is paying to each of his employees.

Behaviors to Use. Direct employees and Systematic bosses are on the same wavelength when it comes to wanting to be efficient in their use of time. However, they may clash when it comes to how to spend that time. Systematic bosses are inclined to schedule time that is focused on analysis and evaluation, while Direct employees are likely to take action and make course corrections along the way. If you are a Direct employee working for a Systematic boss, your boss isn't going to like your "ready, aim, fire" approach. Take a step back and prepare for interactions with your boss with plenty of data and information, presented in a logical manner. Ask rather than tell, and develop your patience to sort through details.

Behaviors to Avoid. To interact effectively with your Systematic boss, refrain from your natural inclination to make snap decisions. Don't present information as fact if it isn't (that is, if it's your opinion or if you can't verify its accuracy). Beware of sounding like you are disagreeing with your boss—you may disagree with the facts, but you should remain diplomatic when interacting with your boss and providing explanations for your point of view.

Systematic Boss, Spirited Employee

Abby works for Kyle in the engineering department of an auto parts manufacturer. Kyle has an excellent track record in developing employees and grooming them to be promoted into

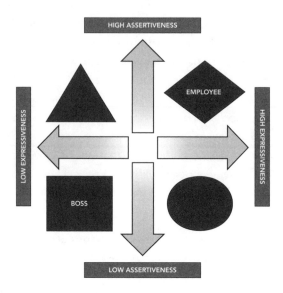

Figure 8.14 **Systematic Boss, Spirited Employee**

management positions. In Abby's case, he sees her potential, but he is concerned about her work style. Abby is a multitasker in a department where a singular but deep focus is more prevalent. From Kyle's perspective, Abby doesn't seem to pay enough attention to the details, which he sees as a significant shortcoming. Her desk is a mess, but she can always find exactly what she's looking for, so Kyle is trying not to let that bother him.

Behaviors to Use. A Spirited employee and a Systematic boss are on opposite sides of the personality style dimensions, so the potential for conflict or tension is high. On the plus side, they can complement each other well—especially if the Spirited employee recognizes the differences and works with them, not against them. If you're a Spirited employee working for a Systematic boss, slow down and stick to the facts. Take a more analytical approach—ouch, but do it! Focus on facts, logic, and details. Make sure you're accurate. Be prepared before meeting with your Systematic boss.

Behaviors to Avoid. Don't show too much emotion or be overly animated—instead of building rapport, this may diminish it. Don't be sloppy, don't appear disorganized, and don't appear unprepared.

Doing any of those things will make your boss question your skills and abilities.

Systematic Boss, Considerate Employee

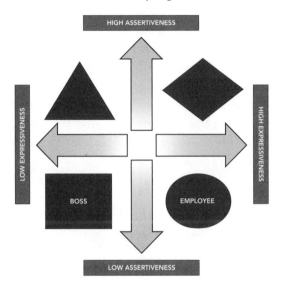

Figure 8.15 **Systematic Boss, Considerate Employee**

David and Stan work for a company that specializes in interactive marketing. Stan supervises David and eight other employees. David is working with Stan to create a new sales forecast. David updates Stan, "I still need to contact two more salespeople to get their estimates before I finish the forecast." Stan replies, "Why do you need to do that? You can just use the formula I developed to calculate potential sales. It will be much more accurate than asking their opinions." David thinks to himself that the employees probably have a more realistic assessment of their potential sales because they can take into account their sense of how close they are to closing a sale, but he is reluctant to contradict Stan because Stan is the boss and David doesn't see any advantage to creating a conflict.

Behaviors to Use. Because they are at opposite ends of the Expressiveness dimension, Considerate employees may have trouble connecting with their Systematic bosses. They may feel rebuffed when they strike up a conversation, and their personal approach may feel invasive to their boss. If you're a Considerate employee working for a Systematic boss, be more formal than usual. Prepare before meeting with your boss. Present your information in a logical manner, and emphasize facts more than feelings. Don't worry about presenting too much information; your boss will appreciate your thoroughness—if the information is well organized.

Behaviors to Avoid. Minimize your socializing and small talk. Avoid surprising your boss; Systematics don't like surprises, even if you think a particular surprise is a good one. Avoid missing deadlines; your boss takes them seriously.

Systematic Boss, Systematic Employee

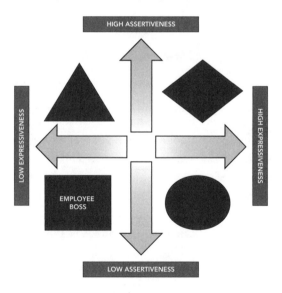

Figure 8.16 **Systematic Boss, Systematic Employee**

Reggie works for Joanne in the billing department of a hospital. Their working relationship is pretty solid; Reggie has worked for Joanne for several years, and they pride themselves on their high accuracy and quality ratings. They are comfortable with the status quo; however, Reggie has heard that a reorganization is in the works throughout the hospital. When he asked Joanne about it, she denied knowing anything about it and changed the subject. Reggie is unsure what to think and is growing increasingly worried about the situation.

Behaviors to Use. Systematic employees working for Systematic bosses obviously have a great deal in common in terms of their work style. Therefore, they are likely to work well together and see eye to eye on how to share information and make decisions—methodically and deliberately! However, since they both tend to keep their feelings to themselves, it may be difficult to develop a working relationship in which either person feels comfortable sharing concerns and stresses. To be most effective, continue to maintain your high standards of quality and accuracy. At the same time, you can support your Systematic boss by breaking free from your comfort zone and gently pushing yourself and your boss to take more risks and make decisions more quickly in order to accomplish even more on behalf of your department or organization.

Behaviors to Avoid. Avoid becoming overly critical, cautious, and conservative, a tendency that may be inadvertently supported by your boss. Avoid getting too bogged down in details, even if that's where you and your boss are comfortable.

EXERCISE: ASSESS YOUR BOSS'S WORK STYLE

Think about recent interactions you've had with your boss. Knowing that your goal is to adjust your own approach to better meet your boss's work style, answer the following questions:

- In what ways is your boss's style most different from yours?

  _____

  _____

- In what situations is that difference most evident?

  _____

  _____

- In what circumstances does the relationship run the most smoothly?

  _____

  _____

- What can you do to minimize friction and maximize compatibility?

  _____

  _____

▶ POINTS TO REMEMBER

▶ You can't change your boss. Therefore, to improve your working relationship, you need to flex your style to meet your boss's preferences.

▶ Issues to consider

- How your boss likes to interact (face to face or electronic; with small talk or all business)

- How your boss makes decisions (quickly or slowly)

- How much information your boss wants from you (just the highlights or a complete analysis)

▶ Tips for dealing with Direct bosses

- _Direct boss/Direct employee:_ Get things done, but keep your boss in the loop.

- _Direct boss/Spirited employee:_ Get to the point quickly; avoid sharing lengthy anecdotes.

- _Direct boss/Considerate employee:_ Limit socializing and focus on results.

- _Direct boss/Systematic employee:_ Speed up decision making and avoid getting bogged down in details.

▶ Tips for dealing with Spirited bosses

- *Spirited boss/Direct employee:* Prioritize your boss's tasks and activities.

- *Spirited boss/Spirited employee:* Avoid letting spontaneous discussions override tasks that must get done.

- *Spirited boss/Considerate employee:* Increase your energy to match your boss's; speak up.

- *Spirited boss/Systematic employee:* Be ready to change gears frequently.

▶ Tips for dealing with Considerate bosses

- *Considerate boss/Direct employee:* Strive for a friendly, relaxed approach with your boss.

- *Considerate boss/Spirited employee:* Focus on one thing at a time when interacting with your boss.

- *Considerate boss/Considerate employee:* Avoid burying conflict that may cause resentment later.

- *Considerate boss/Systematic employee:* Take the time to share your feelings and concerns with your boss.

▶ Tips for dealing with Systematic bosses

- *Systematic boss/Direct employee:* Refrain from making snap decisions; keep your boss in the loop.

- *Systematic boss/Spirited employee:* Slow down and stick to the facts.

- *Systematic boss/Considerate employee:* Be more formal than usual.

- *Systematic boss/Systematic employee:* Avoid being overly critical, cautious, or conservative.

PART IV

USING PERSONALITY STYLES TO ADVANCE YOUR CAREER

Nine

PLANT WHERE
YOU'LL BLOOM

t would be hard to argue that our career choices are not profoundly influenced by the era in which we happen to be born. For example, someone born in the 1920s or early 1930s probably used wholly different criteria to evaluate his career choices from someone born in the 1950s, 1960s, 1970s, or 1980s.

Depending on the prevailing social, cultural, and economic influences of your own era, you might have dreamed of becoming an astronaut, a rock star, a crusading journalist, or a professional athlete. On the other hand, the cultural and economic conditions of your particular era might also have pushed you toward a safer, more rational career, such as becoming a doctor, a lawyer, a teacher, an accountant, or a banking executive.

No matter how you ended up in your current job or why—whether because of direct socioeconomic factors or pure serendipity—there's no reason why you should dread going to work on Monday.

This chapter will help you figure out how you can draw on your natural strengths so that you end up doing less of the activities that you don't do well (or have the least interest in doing) and more of the things that will help you look forward to your work when the alarm clock rings on Monday morning. The compromise may not be exactly the same as reporting to NASA for a mission to Mars or hearing the incredible riff you just executed on your guitar reverberating around a sold-out concert hall, but for most of us it's a pretty good deal.

Making the Match—Job, Culture, and Work Environment

First off, you need to understand that a job/personality mismatch does not preclude a person from holding or even being successful in a particular job. On the other hand, certain professions are particularly well suited to each of the personality styles discussed in this book. For example, counselors are often Considerates, engineers are frequently Systematics, police officers are often Directs, and many salespeople are Spiriteds.

One of the goals of this book is to help you find that perfect match that enables you to feel energized every morning when you go to work, proud when you describe your work to others, valued for your contributions, and focused on a positive future. What follows is a pathway to help you assemble the two parts to a good match: the particular job you do and the culture or work environment of the organization in which you do it. Once you fully understand the requirements of such a match, options are revealed that help you see opportunities to make a career change, or perhaps even to choose to remain in the same occupation but change your work setting.

Julie graduated from college with a major in marketing. Her first job out of college was working for a consumer goods company. Julie started as an assistant to a product manager. She had many duties, including coordinating meetings, planning special events, and arranging photo shoots. Julie was ambivalent about her job; she saw how excited some of her coworkers were about what they did, but she just didn't feel it—except when she was attending photo shoots. She loved every minute of those and pitched in to help arrange the set and the products being shot. Julie realized that she was more interested in interior design than in marketing, so she went back to school and got a second degree in interior design. Even though the field is highly competitive and doesn't pay well unless you're a top designer, Julie is happy in her new occupation, using her creativity to bring joy to her clients.

CULTURE QUIZ

The key to finding the ideal career and work setting is to know yourself; that's why so much of this chapter is devoted to asking questions. As you move through the chapter, take the time to reflect on the following questions and consider your answers carefully. The questions are open-ended and have no right or wrong answers. They are simply designed to lead you toward finding a fulfilling occupation in a satisfying work environment.

- What activities make you feel energized? _____

  _____

- What activities drain your energy? _____

  _____

- What activities come naturally or easily to you? _____

  _____

- What activities do you struggle to complete? _____

  _____

- If you could do any job in your life, what would you choose?

  _____

  _____

- What fulfillment do you seek from the work itself? _____

  _____

  _____

  _____

- In what areas do your friends, family, and colleagues see you as an expert? _____

  _____

- What do people ask you to help them with? _____

  _____

- What areas or subjects are you interested in, but perhaps haven't had the opportunity to pursue? _____

  _____

- Have your friends or family ever said, "You should do _____"?
  If so, what area did they say it of? _____
  _____

- Based on your answers, can you identify a theme or pattern for
  your career or your potential new career? _____
  _____
  _____

SKILLS INVENTORY

Instructions: For each skill listed, rate your ability at it and your interest in it, using the following scale: 1 = none, 2 = a little, 3 = some, 4 = extremely high.

Skill	Ability (1–4)	Interest (1–4)	Total Score
1. Delegating	_____	_____	_____
2. Instructing others	_____	_____	_____
3. Coaching	_____	_____	_____
4. Counseling	_____	_____	_____
5. Motivating others	_____	_____	_____
6. Directing	_____	_____	_____
7. Public speaking	_____	_____	_____
8. Writing	_____	_____	_____
9. Negotiating	_____	_____	_____
10. Presenting ideas	_____	_____	_____
11. Editing	_____	_____	_____
12. Facilitation	_____	_____	_____

Skill	Ability (1–4)	Interest (1–4)	Total Score
13. Listening			
14. Handling complaints			
15. Managing conflict			
16. Selling			
17. Team building			
18. Fund-raising			
19. Setting priorities			
20. Managing details			
21. Conceptualizing			
22. Reviewing			
23. Making decisions			
24. Budgeting			
25. Scheduling			

Assessment

List the three skills on which you scored the highest:

1. _____
2. _____
3. _____

List the three skills on which you scored the lowest:

1. _____
2. _____
3. _____

Obviously, when you are considering a job or a career, you want to choose one that draws on your preferences and strengths while avoiding the tasks where you have less ability and interest.

OCCUPATIONS FOR THE DIFFERENT PERSONALITY STYLES

In this section, you'll learn about the typical strengths and prefer- ences of people with each personality style, and discover a few of the careers that are a good match for people with each style. Keep in mind that we can't list every possible occupation; we'll just give you a few ideas as a jumping-off point. In addition, remember that people with every style can do every job; the goal is to find the ideal job and work environment for you, based on your personality style and your individual preferences.

People with the Direct Style

If your personality style is Direct, these terms describe you: assertive, ambitious, demanding, decisive, competitive, and risk taker.

> Tamara is the CEO of an online retailer of activewear for women. Under her leadership, the company has gained mar- ket share and increased its profit margins. She is especially pleased that the company recently overtook a competitor and is now the dominant player in its market segment. Tamara finds the daily demands of leading a company challenging—while no two days are the same, she prefers strategic planning and goal setting to actively managing others and dealing with per- sonnel issues. She wishes the members of her staff could be more like her—self-starters who take the initiative and have the drive to succeed.

Tamara likes her job because she gets to be in charge, make deci- sions, and see the results of those decisions. She has the opportunity to set goals and achieve them, and to earn respect and recognition for her accomplishments. She relishes being in a position of author- ity and control.

Other characteristics of a job that people with the Direct style find fulfilling are the chance to meet and interact with other powerful and capable people, the opportunity to be in the public eye (recognized and rewarded for their accomplishments), the ability to advance within the organization, the opportunity to work on and solve or overcome complex or difficult problems, and the ability to supervise others without getting mired in interpersonal conflicts.

The business world is a likely place to find a career that matches those qualities. The sidebar includes other ideas for people with the Direct style. Remember, this list is not exhaustive.

OCCUPATIONS FOR PEOPLE WITH A DIRECT STYLE

These are just a few of the occupations that could be fulfilling to individuals with a Direct style.

- Entrepreneur
- CEO or executive management
- Sales and sales management
- Franchise owner or operator
- Investment banking
- Stockbroker
- Venture capitalist
- Controller
- Pilot
- Law enforcement
- Paramedic/EMT
- Attorney
- University professor or administrator

EXERCISE: JOB OPPORTUNITIES FOR DIRECT-STYLE INDIVIDUALS

If you have a Direct style, what possible occupations appeal to you based on your answers to the culture quiz questions and the information about the Direct style? _____

_____

_____

People with the Spirited Style

If you have a Spirited style, people describe you as being outgoing, creative, enthusiastic, optimistic, and dramatic.

> Brett is the VP of business and economic development for a major metropolitan chamber of commerce. He describes his job like this: "I give my opinions and advice, and people act on my ideas!" Among his recent accomplishments, Brett created a consortium of almost 100 organizations to serve as ambassadors to site selectors and business representatives considering a move to the city, to share the advantages of locating their businesses in the city. In addition, Brett has been working to raise awareness about several ballot initiatives in the upcoming election that have the potential to hinder business growth in the community.

Brett loves his job because it enables him to interact with a diverse group of powerful movers and shakers in the community. He is presented with a myriad of challenges, and he gets great satisfaction out of developing innovative solutions to these problems. As a bonus, he has reached a point in his career where he has staff members to handle the details of his projects.

Other job characteristics that will appeal to you as a Spirited: you love to talk to people, but you don't like to get bogged down in red tape or bureaucracy; you crave variety and thrive on having many different projects and activities going on at once; you like to meet new people and learn new things; and you want to work with a minimum of rules and regulations to restrain you. You are friendly and upbeat, and you want others to be the same way.

Brett has found his ideal job. Because of their innate creativity, Spiriteds are likely to be attracted to jobs in the arts—review the additional career ideas for people with the Spirited style in the sidebar. Because people with the Spirited style desire variety, they are the most likely style to change jobs and occupations multiple times over the course of their working career.

OCCUPATIONS FOR PEOPLE
WITH A SPIRITED STYLE

These are just a few of the occupations that could be fulfilling to individuals with a Spirited style.

- Jobs in the arts: musician, actor, photographer, artist, writer
- Interior designer
- Graphic designer
- Newspaper columnist/blogger
- Video game developer
- Public relations executive
- Advertising and marketing manager
- High school guidance counselor
- Politician

EXERCISE: JOB OPPORTUNITIES FOR SPIRITED-STYLE INDIVIDUALS

If you have a Spirited style, what possible occupations appeal to you based on your answers to the culture quiz questions and the information about the Spirited style? _____

_____

_____

_____

People with the Considerate Style

If your personality style preference is Considerate, these terms describe you: cooperative, dependable, a good listener, avoids conflict, negotiator, and supportive.

> Oscar is a genetic counselor for a nonprofit agency that assists individuals and couples dealing with genetic disorders. His typical day is a combination of working on his own or with colleagues evaluating family history and medical data, and meeting with clients, often pregnant women or new parents who are struggling to absorb and understand devastating news. One of Oscar's strengths is translating technical medical jargon into plain language that the client can understand. He does this with compassion and clarity. Though his job can be emotionally exhausting, Oscar gains satisfaction from knowing that he is helping clients in a time of need.

Oscar finds his job fulfilling because he develops meaningful relationships with others; in fact, his clients often stay in touch with him long past the end of their official or formal interactions. In addition, his job requires him to have the ability to be supportive and affirming, which he does well.

Additional characteristics of occupations that will appeal to Considerates include having a sense of purpose and meaning, creating an atmosphere of cooperation and harmony, offering practical help and handling details that have concrete results, having the ability to work at your own pace and in your own way, not being tied to pointless rules and regulations, having the opportunity to collaborate with others, and not having to do public speaking in front of large groups of people you don't know.

Oscar's job is a good fit for him. Review the sidebar on the next page for other ideas that suit people with a Considerate style.

EXERCISE: JOB OPPORTUNITIES FOR CONSIDERATE-STYLE INDIVIDUALS

If you have a Considerate style, what possible occupations appeal to you based on your answers to the culture quiz questions and the information about the Considerate style? _____

_____

_____

_____

OCCUPATIONS FOR PEOPLE WITH A CONSIDERATE STYLE

These are just a few of the occupations that could be fulfilling to individuals with a Considerate style.

- Physician (especially pediatrician or family practice)
- Nurse
- Physical or occupational therapist
- Speech language pathologist
- Dietitian
- Hospice director
- Teacher
- Childcare provider
- Customer service representative
- Social worker
- Counselor
- Clergy member
- Paralegal
- Office manager
- Event planner

People with the Systematic Style

If your personality style is Systematic, you know that these adjectives describe you: logical, organized, methodical, precise, analytical, rational, and efficient.

> Stephanie is an attorney working in the risk management department of a large financial institution. Her regular work responsibilities include reviewing contracts and other legal documents, researching and evaluating proposed business decisions, and developing contingency plans to prepare for unexpected or crisis situations. Stephanie finds satisfaction in developing and adhering to strict standards that uphold the excellent performance of the financial institution. She knows that her work contributes to the value of the organization, and that her skills are specialized and necessary to the success of the company.

Stephanie enjoys her job because she has a great deal of autonomy, and she is given the time and space she needs to complete her work carefully and accurately.

Other traits that appeal to people with a Systematic style: you want to deal in facts, not feelings; you prefer to work independently rather than in a team; you want a clearly defined organizational structure with specific goals and objectives; you like having a specialized skill set that you can apply to real (not theoretical) problems and situations; you want the ability to grow and advance based on achieving stated results or meeting stated expectations; and you want to be rewarded for thoughtful analysis and efficient operating procedures. Not surprisingly, occupations that suit the Systematic style have similar characteristics. Review the sidebar for some suggestions.

OCCUPATIONS FOR PEOPLE WITH A SYSTEMATIC STYLE

These are just a few of the occupations that could be fulfilling to individuals with a Systematic style.

- Business administrator
- Accountant
- Logistics and supply manager
- Database administrator
- Programmer
- Systems analyst
- Financial analyst
- Insurance underwriter

- Engineer (mechanical, civil, electrical, or some other specialty)
- Detective
- Judge
- Construction/building inspector
- Military officer
- Flight engineer/ navigator
- Dentist

Exercise: Job Opportunities for Systematic-Style Individuals

If you have a Systematic style, what possible occupations appeal to you based on your answers to the culture quiz questions and the information about the Systematic style? _____

_____

_____

_____

Choosing a Work Setting

Just as people have different personality styles, organizations have different styles, too. An organization's style or culture is influenced by many factors—by the person or people who started the organization, by its current leaders, and by the surrounding geographic and societal conventions, as well as by the nature of the work it does.

Clashing with your organization's culture can result in job dissatisfaction, even if you like your occupation. According to the founder of the Center for Values Research, Dr. Charles Hughes, harmonious personal and organization values increase an employee's desire to stay with an organization, whereas differences in values decrease an employee's desire to stay.[1] Therefore, finding an occupation that suits your personality style *and* finding a compatible work setting are two major factors in job satisfaction.

Having compatible cultures is also a factor when two organizations merge. That's why it can be so difficult for two companies to merge successfully. The *Wall Street Journal* reported on the failure of the partnership between Volkswagen and Suzuki: "Volkswagen Chief Executive Martin Winterkorn in March said slow decision making at Suzuki was responsible for the partnership's lack of progress. 'We here in the Western world are sometimes more decisive than in Japan's more consensus-oriented culture, he said.'"[2]

A study sponsored by the Society for Human Resource Management and conducted by Towers Perrin, titled "Making Mergers

Work," found that HR professionals listed "incompatible cultures" as among the biggest obstacles to success in mergers and acquisitions.[3]

Thus, it's important to take the time to find the ideal organizational culture for your personality style.

EXERCISE: WORKPLACE VALUES ASSESSMENT

Read each description and rate how important it is to you to have this characteristic in your workplace environment, using a scale of 1 to 4 with the following meanings: 1 = doesn't matter, not important at all; 2 = somewhat important to me; 3 = quite important to me; 4 = must have, extremely important to me.

_____ 1. Order and structure

_____ 2. High degree of competition

_____ 3. Flexibility in work structure

_____ 4. Loyalty

_____ 5. Self-respect and pride in work

_____ 6. Strong financial compensation and rewards

_____ 7. Public recognition for contributions

_____ 8. Stability and security

_____ 9. Independence and autonomy

_____ 10. Opportunity for power and leadership

_____ 11. Creativity

_____ 12. Warm working relationships

_____ 13. High standards of quality

_____ 14. Clear opportunities for advancement

_____ 15. Variety in tasks and projects

_____ 16. Teamwork and collaboration

Scoring

Total for questions 1, 5, 9, and 13: _____. If this total is the highest, it indicates a preference for a Systematic work environment.

Total for questions 2, 6, 10, and 14: _____. If this total is the highest, it indicates a preference for a Direct work environment.

Total for questions 3, 7, 11, and 15: _____. If this total is the highest, it indicates a preference for a Spirited work environment.

Total for questions 4, 8, 12, and 16: _____. If this total is the highest, it indicates a preference for a Considerate work environment.

DESCRIPTION OF ORGANIZATION CULTURES

James, Miguel, Lilly, and Tina are all doctors who attended the same medical school. They all did their residencies in pediatric care. All four physicians share the same occupation, but in very different settings, and they all find their careers fulfilling and are eager to go to work each day.

Working in a Direct Culture

James owns a thriving pediatric practice. He works long hours and enjoys the financial rewards of his hard work. He employs three doctors in his practice, along with a staff of four nurses and three front-office employees. He is also the president of his state's professional association of pediatric physicians. James prides himself that his practice is the largest in his community, and that it has a reputation for offering a high level of quality and professionalism. Over the years, James has worked hard to improve his "bedside manner," especially when interacting with patients and families with serious medical issues.

If you work in a Direct style environment, like James's, you will find an emphasis on taking action and achieving results. It will be a competitive environment, with colleagues being almost rivals. However, the rewards for individual effort and accomplishments are great. The organization constantly seeks challenges and values risk taking. So, if you are a reluctant risk taker and prefer to avoid conflict, this may not be the environment for you.

EXERCISE: WHERE TO LOOK FOR A DIRECT CULTURE

If the Direct culture seems like a good fit for you, here are some questions you could ask when interviewing or shadowing to determine whether this organization might be the right place for you.

* What would you say your organization values? (In a Direct environment, you should hear answers such as decisiveness, results, and risk taking.)

* Would you say your organization values teamwork or individual accomplishment more? (A Direct environment values individual effort.)

* How are decisions made in this organization? (A Direct culture makes decisions quickly, based on gut reactions and instinct.)

* Other questions you would like to ask: _____
  _____
  _____
  _____

Working in a Spirited Culture

Miguel works at a university teaching hospital in a major metropolitan city. This hospital has developed a reputation for specializing in pediatric respiratory disorders, including allergies, asthma, and cystic fibrosis. Miguel is the chief of pediatrics and splits his time among seeing patients, teaching students and residents, and speaking at medical conferences. Patients and their families are generally from all over the country, and Miguel's consultations with them are usually just for one or two appointments. He enjoys the recognition he receives from his position and from his speaking engagements.

If you work in a Spirited style culture, like Miguel's, you will notice the high energy and nearly frenetic pace. Colleagues are enthusiastic and optimistic, and innovation is highly valued. The atmosphere is extremely social and fun, and group activities outside of work are regular events. Communication is frequent (some would say too frequent—expect many lengthy meetings in a Spirited culture). In addition, the organization may change focus and direction frequently, and you may get frustrated if the Spirited style isn't for you.

 ### Exercise: Where to Look for a Spirited Culture

If the Spirited culture seems like a good fit for you, here are some questions you could ask when interviewing or shadowing to determine whether this organization might be the right place for you.

- What would you say your organization values? (In a Spirited environment, you should hear answers such as creativity, innovation, enthusiasm, and optimism.)

- Would you say your organization values teamwork or individual accomplishment more? (A Spirited environment values teamwork and collaboration.)

- How are decisions made in this organization? (A Spirited culture makes decisions quickly, based on intuition and the persuasive skills of others.)

- Other questions you would like to ask: _____
  _____
  _____
  _____

Working in a Considerate Culture

Lilly works at a not-for-profit community clinic. Its stated mission is to serve low-income and uninsured residents, delivering care that is prevention-focused and culturally appropriate. It sees itself as a safety net for a population that might otherwise receive no care or use the emergency room for its care. Lilly has developed long-lasting relationships, both with her colleagues and with her patients. She enjoys seeing babies grow into young adults and seeing their parents gain knowledge and experience in how to raise healthy children.

If you work in a Considerate style culture, like Lilly's, you will notice that the company offers a supportive environment, both to its staff and to its customers or clients. It offers an opportunity to form collaborative relationships, both within and outside the organization. The atmosphere is generally more relaxed than that in other styles, and there is an emphasis on harmony and getting along with others. However, if you are highly assertive and desire recognition and advancement based on individual accomplishments and results, a Considerate culture may not be for you.

 ### EXERCISE: WHERE TO LOOK FOR A CONSIDERATE CULTURE

If the Considerate culture seems like a good fit for you, here are some questions you could ask when interviewing or shadowing to determine whether this organization might be the right place for you.

- What would you say your organization values? (In a Considerate environment, you should hear answers such as harmony, cooperation, support, and loyalty.)

- Would you say your organization values teamwork or individual accomplishment more? (A Considerate environment values teamwork and collaboration.)

- How are decisions made in this organization? (A Considerate culture makes decisions slowly, after collecting input from many people and sources.)

- Other questions you would like to ask: _____

_____

_____

Working in a Systematic Culture

Tina works at the university associated with the teaching hospital. She is one of the lead researchers specializing in cystic fibrosis. She has one close colleague with whom she does most of her research, and then a wide circle of associates and acquaintances. She and her research partner are about to publish the results of cutting-edge research, and she has spent many hours writing, reviewing, and editing the article. She is looking forward to the recognition that she and her partner will receive for their research, and she expects to receive additional funding for their research as a result.

If you work in a Systematic style culture, like Tina's, you will find a stable environment. Your colleagues will be punctual and dependable, and will maintain high standards of performance. The pace will be slower; for example, decisions are made after lengthy analysis, and are based on logic and data. The Systematic culture is detail-oriented and expects precision and accuracy. It is basically free from emotions, so if you desire a social group that works closely together, this may not be the place for you.

EXERCISE: WHERE TO LOOK FOR A SYSTEMATIC CULTURE

If the Systematic culture seems like a good fit for you, here are some questions you could ask when interviewing or shadowing to determine whether this organization might be the right place for you.

- What would you say your organization values? (In a Systematic environment, you should hear answers such as logic, accuracy, dependability, and quality.)

- Would you say your organization values teamwork or individual accomplishment more? (A Systematic environment values independence and autonomy.)

- How are decisions made in this organization? (A Systematic culture makes decisions slowly, after thorough analysis.)
- Other questions you would like to ask: _____

_____

_____

CUSTOMIZING YOUR JOB SEARCH

The U.S. Bureau of Labor Statistics (BLS) economist Chuck Pierret conducted a study about job stability and, based on interviews with 10,000 people, found that the people interviewed held 10.8 jobs, on average, between the ages of 18 and 42. Another statistic from the same study found that the average tenure of an American worker is 4.1 years, based on 2008 data.[4] Either way you look at it, people are changing jobs relatively frequently.

If you find yourself in an occupation or a work culture that you want to change, then you need to search for a new job. People with each personality style will go about their job hunt in a different way. While it's natural to stick with your strengths and preferences, you will be most successful if you use strategies from all four styles.

Direct Job Search

Since you are action-oriented and assertive (not to mention competitive), you will be in a hurry to get a new job. This can work both for you and against you. On the plus side, you won't wait around for people to contact you or respond to your inquiries—you will call them directly. However, some people will see this as pushy or too demanding and may develop a negative opinion of you. Your impatience may also lead you to shortchange the time you spend writing cover letters and e-mails and polishing your résumé.

To make the most of your job-hunting effort, develop some patience. Take the time to create a top-notch résumé that accurately reflects your accomplishments. When you meet with a prospective employer, show him that you can really listen. Avoid alienating people by being too pushy in your conversation. The positive side of your results-oriented nature will reveal itself without your having to point it out. And one more thought—don't abandon your job search if you don't get the immediate results you're looking for. Be patient with yourself, and be willing to wait for the ideal opportunity.

Spirited Job Search

You are energetic and optimistic, two important qualities in a successful job search. You also have a large network of contacts and love talking to them, so you are likely to uncover some opportunities through serendipity. On the other hand, since you are interested in so many different things, you may become easily distracted from the tasks necessary to complete a successful job search, such as doing research, filling out applications, and writing a polished, mistake-free résumé. Or you may change your mind frequently about the path you want to take, making it difficult for you to follow through on your desire to change jobs. In addition, your aversion to handling details may result in your submitting sloppy applications and cover letters and résumés with mistakes and typos, leaving a poor impression on potential employers.

Overcome these tendencies by organizing your job search—enlist professional help, if necessary, and be open to criticism in order to improve both your résumé and your interviewing skills. Get the details right, and let your creativity and enthusiasm shine.

Considerate Job Search

You have a calm demeanor and an easygoing temperament. You are friendly with everyone and a great listener. These are all qualities that make you a valuable employee; however, they can hold you back from getting hired for your ideal job, as you may not make a strong impression on potential employers. In fact, your reluctance to change may hold you back from even looking for your ideal job.

However, you have good organizational and follow-through skills that will help you launch and persist in your job search. In order to make your job hunt successful, follow these tips:

> *Up your energy level.* It may feel uncomfortable and artificial to you, but to others you'll appear eager and interested in the position.

> *Develop an "elevator speech."* This is a short summary of your skills and accomplishments and why you should be considered

for the position. Practice it ahead of time so that you'll sound confident and persuasive.

Actively network with others. Ask for the names of people you can contact from friends, friends of friends, and even prospective employers who have turned you down for a particular job. Your likability will open doors for you, if you just put a little effort into it.

Systematic Job Search

You are strong in research and analysis. You are also a stickler for accuracy and details, making you skilled at writing flawless résumés, cover letters, and e-mail inquiries. However, your need to analyze both potential new career paths and specific positions thoroughly may slow down your job hunt.

You may spend too much time researching and not enough time networking to conduct an effective job campaign. In addition, your thoughtful, analytical nature may be perceived as critical and flat in an interview. Your job search will require you to step out of your comfort zone and be more assertive, both in networking with potential employers and in presenting yourself in interviews.

Learn to trust your instincts about a potential job instead of relying solely on logic. And try not to obsess about unimportant details of your job hunt if doing so prevents you from moving forward and making progress. Your consistency and high standards will be apparent in your presentation of yourself, both on paper and in person.

EXERCISE: IMPROVE YOUR JOB SEARCH STRATEGIES

What is your job search (personality) style? _____

_____

What do you see as your strongest job-hunting skill, based on your personality style? _____

_____

_____

What do you see as your primary job-hunting weakness, based on your personality style? _____

_____

What are some strengths or strategies from other styles that you would like to adopt in your job search? _____

_____

_____

▶ POINTS TO REMEMBER

- ▶ The ideal job for you matches your personality style, both in the particular work you do and in the setting in which you do it.

- ▶ Complete a detailed culture quiz to determine the most fulfilling occupations for you.

- ▶ Direct style occupations take advantage of your natural strengths of being decisive and taking risks, and they reward individual accomplishments.

- ▶ Spirited style occupations take advantage of your natural strengths of interacting with a wide variety of people and tasks and of being enthusiastic and optimistic, and they offer recognition for creativity and innovation.

- ▶ Considerate style occupations take advantage of your natural strengths of developing collaborative relationships and being supportive and affirming, and they offer a sense of purpose and meaning.

- ▶ Systematic style occupations take advantage of your natural strengths of accuracy and analysis, allow you to be organized and methodical, and reward achieving the highest standards of quality.

- ▶ Direct style work environments offer a high degree of competition, strong financial compensation and rewards, and clear opportunities for advancement.

▶ Spirited style work environments offer flexibility in work structure, variety in tasks and projects, and public recognition for contributions.

▶ Considerate style work environments offer stability, security, loyalty, teamwork, and collaboration.

▶ Systematic style work environments offer order and structure, independence and autonomy, and they provide self-respect and pride in your work.

Ten

BLOOM WHERE YOU'RE PLANTED

S o what impact do personality and style differences among individual workers have on job satisfaction and contentment on the job?

Aiden and Zack are coworkers in the quality control department of a manufacturer of musical instruments. Aiden is quite settled in his position; he enjoys the attention to detail that his position requires, and he likes working on his own. On the other hand, Zack is constantly frustrated by his job. Though he likes handling the instruments, he finds the work too solitary, and he misses the camaraderie with coworkers that he's experienced in other jobs.

The answer is found in the degree to which these individuals are able to find common ground, adapt, and change in ways that allow them to coexist with the organizational and cultural styles of the organization that is signing their paychecks.

IDENTIFY YOUR ORGANIZATION'S CULTURE

In the previous chapter, you learned to identify the ideal work environment for people with your personality style. You also learned that organizations, like individual workers, have their own distinct styles. This chapter will examine how you can make the most of your own individual style even when your style and the style of your organization seem to be directly at odds. For most of us, the ability to "bloom where you're planted" may be the most important job skill we can possess—especially if leaving our job is not an option.

Before getting started, it's a good idea to think about your organization's culture and its overall style as discussed and defined previously in this book by looking at the assertiveness and expressiveness dimensions of your organization. Is your organization fast paced? Does your organization value quick decision making, or does it value slower, deliberate decision making?

If you think your organization falls into the faster-paced category, then you probably work in a Direct or Spirited organization. If you consider your organization to be slower paced, then it's likely that you work in a Systematic or Considerate organization.

Now think about how employees in your organization communicate with one another. Is the communication short and to the point, or is lengthy, idea-sharing communication encouraged? Short and sweet communication indicates that you work in a company with a Direct or Systematic style. If your organization values more lengthy, idea-sharing communication, then your company has a Spirited or Considerate style.

To determine the style of your organization, simply put the two dimensions together and you should have a fairly accurate picture of your organization's style.

If you're having trouble identifying your organization's style even after this exercise, here's a way to further sharpen your focus.

What behaviors does your organization reward? For example, does your organization reward individual results or results achieved through collaboration? If your organization is focused on individual results, then it probably has a Direct style. If collaboration and teamwork are the focus, then you work in an organization with a Considerate style.

A further indicator to help you identify your organization's style includes an examination of whether it rewards ideas or analysis. A Spirited organization may focus more on creative, out-of-the-box ideas. A more Systematic organization prefers logic and methodical analysis to drive decisions.

Use Table 10.1 as a tool to help you further refine your analysis and determine your own organization's style.

Style	Direct	Spirited	Considerate	Systematic
Behaviors	Results Decisiveness Success Competition	Creativity Enthusiasm Optimism Fun	Teamwork Harmony Compassion Loyalty	Quality Accuracy Dependability Objectivity

Table 10.1 Characteristics of Organization Styles

WORKING WITH ORGANIZATIONAL STYLE

One of the best ways to learn and apply concepts is through the experience of others. The rest of this chapter consists of four case studies, each describing a different organization with a different style and culture. As you read through these examples, think about how well the situations described mirror your own experiences and the culture and style of your own organization.

At the end of each case study, you'll find a set of questions that allow you to determine whether or not that particular case study is an appropriate match to your own organization's culture and style. Once you've determined a match, then your detailed answers to these questions, along with the insight you gained from reading the case study, become the "soil" you need if you are to truly "bloom where you are planted."

DBG: HOW'S YOUR FIT?

DBG was started as Double Beta Games, which was shortened to DBG as the company's products gained popularity and recognition. It is one of the cutting-edge video game developers. In the first years of its existence, it was growing at 200 percent annually. Growth has slowed, but it is still steady at 10 percent per year. The founder of DBG has an MBA from a top business school. His philosophy is that to be the best, you have to hire the best, and then let competition weed out the less than best. His leadership style can be summed up by the fact that his favorite movie is *Gladiator*.

The company has a straightforward structure; it is basically organized into product teams, each of which includes a producer (the team manager), programmers, graphic artists, sound engineers, and testers. Support units—sales and marketing, HR, accounting, and other such functions—round out the hierarchy. People in these units are routinely treated as second-class citizens in the company.

Brett, one of the video development managers, describes working at DBG as challenging, in both the positive and the negative sense. For example, pitch sessions for new game ideas can be brutal, as everyone else in the room seeks to shoot down your idea and promote his own. On the other hand, Brett firmly believes that applying this ruthless approach to evaluating potential new games has helped DBG create the most successful games.

Quarterly monetary awards are given out to the best-performing employees. This has created a highly competitive environment in which individuals are unwilling to share insights and shortcuts with others—even if they could increase the overall performance of the organization—because they fear that doing so will decrease their chances of winning the individual performance award.

Direct style. If you have a Direct style, you will feel comfortable working in a Direct-style environment like DBG (see the sidebar for a brief review of the Direct culture). However, if you do not have a Direct style, you may feel tense or unhappy working in such an environment. We'll look at how you can adjust your style to maximize your strengths and minimize conflicts with others while working in a Direct setting.

Spirited style. If you have a Spirited style and you are working in a Direct culture, you are likely to experience some or all of the following reactions. You may

- Enjoy the speed at which the organization operates.

- Find that your energy matches the pace of the environment.

- See how your creativity and innovative ideas immediately benefit the organization.

On the other hand, you may

- Feel that your ideas are not acknowledged.

DIRECT CULTURE REVIEW

The Direct organization

- Values decisiveness, action, and results.

- Encourages competition.

- Rewards individual accomplishments.

- Seeks challenges.

- Celebrates victories.

- Looks for independent thinkers and risk takers.

Downsides

- Constant competition may lead to stress and burnout.

- Power struggles may develop.

- Others may put you down in order to get ahead.

- Emphasis on quick action may lead to poor decisions.

- Lack of thorough analysis may ultimately hurt the organization.

- Fail to receive recognition that you feel you deserve because in a Direct culture, the expectation is that you are simply doing your job.

- Find it difficult to persuade your Direct colleagues to agree with your point of view, as they probably have strong views of their own.

To make the most of your Spirited strengths in a Direct culture, selectively choose the ideas that you want to promote—focus on the ones that can produce results most quickly and easily. Narrow your attention so that you don't appear scattered to others. You may also need to tone down your emotions to relate better to your less emotional colleagues. For example, if pitching ideas or proposals is part of your job, prepare in advance by anticipating arguments against your idea and having your responses ready.

Considerate style. If you have a Considerate style and you are working in a Direct environment, you are at the opposite end of both the assertiveness and the expressiveness dimensions. The highly competitive, individual achievement focus of a Direct organization is the opposite of your preference for collaboration and teamwork. Thus, you will have to make more adjustments to fit into your work environment. You are likely to experience any or all of the following reactions. You may

- Feel constantly anxious because of both the lack of information and the blunt approach to addressing conflict.

- Feel hurt by real or perceived slights.

On the other hand, you may

- Find that your Considerate strengths and qualities help balance out the assertive Direct environment.

- Be counted on by your colleagues to be a good listener and provide support.

- Help relax the atmosphere with your low-key demeanor.

To survive and thrive in a Direct culture when you have a Considerate style, you need to develop a thicker skin. You have to realize that in this culture, no news is good news, so you shouldn't expect to receive much feedback. Reach out to a small handful of colleagues for support and encouragement rather than looking for it throughout the organization. In the DBG example, you could suggest opportunities for connecting the different product teams and building unity throughout the organization. You could even approach HR to change the award structure to reward the overall performance of the organization rather than individuals or individual teams.

Systematic style. If you have a Systematic style and you are working in a Direct culture, you may have one or more of the following reactions. You may

- Feel comfortable in the businesslike, task-focused atmosphere.

- Consider the lack of small talk and socializing a good thing.

- Like the emphasis on independent achievement and results.

On the other hand, you may

- Feel anxious because of the degree of competitiveness.

- Get stressed out by what you consider to be hasty decision making.

- Feel frustrated by the "ready, aim, fire" approach in a Direct culture.

- Find that your desire for thorough analysis and 100 percent accuracy isn't appreciated.

To make the most of your Systematic style strengths in a Direct culture, your best bet is to offer some give and take—pick one or two critical decisions that will have the greatest impact on the organization and ask for the time you need for a full analysis of those decisions. Then, allow other decisions to be made with less complete analysis. Chances are, you will still provide your colleagues with enough information for them to feel comfortable taking action. For example, at DBG, you could get involved in the game testing and develop a template that would enable all testers to follow a thorough plan to ensure that all bugs are caught.

EXERCISE: ADAPT TO THE DIRECT CULTURE

Now that you have an idea of how the other three personality styles can fit into or clash with a Direct organizational culture, apply any lessons learned to your own work situation. If you work in a Direct culture, then work through the following questions to begin developing your own set of action items to better align your personality style with those of your team and your organization. Think carefully about the answers to these questions. Remember, it's a good idea to jot down your initial impressions and thoughts in a notebook (paper or electronic) for future reference.

- How could you help Spiriteds gain the creativity and blue-sky thinking they thrive on?

- How could you help Considerates feel connected to their colleagues?

- How could you help Systematics carve out time to use their logical, analytical approach?

TALUMBRE: HOW'S YOUR FIT?

Talumbre is a relatively new company that sells specialized medical equipment. It was founded by two women who began their careers as engineers, moved into sales, and then got interested in product design. They received funding from an angel investor who was heavily involved in the initial development of the business plan and in obtaining appropriate resources to get the business off the ground.

Sales of the company's initial equipment have been good, and now the founders want to develop another related piece of equipment. However, they are having trouble settling on a design. They have consulted with their current customers and have found disparate opinions about the exact best design. So far, they've held lots of brainstorming meetings and developed prototypes, but they are not close to getting the design approved to begin manufacturing and testing.

The investor has stepped back out of daily operations at this point, and the founders are discovering that running a profitable business is very different from creating one. They have spent the majority of their time focused on new product development, and they realize that someone needs to pay more attention to their current product.

Leslie, a new employee, describes working at Talumbre as exhilarating on a good day and exhausting on a bad day. She loves the usually upbeat, optimistic environment and appreciates the recognition she receives for her contributions and innovations. However, sometimes the atmosphere is chaotic, and the constant changes can make her feel less productive. And she has noticed that the "realists" in the company—those who bring up possible negative consequences of ideas and decisions—are considered to be drags. She wonders if the lack of a balanced perspective may come back to haunt the company in some way in the future.

If you have a Spirited style, you will probably feel at home at Talumbre or in other Spirited environments (see the sidebar for a brief review of the Spirited culture). However, if you do not have a Spirited style, you may wonder how any work gets done with all the talking and socializing. Making small changes in your own work style will go a long way toward increasing your job satisfaction when you are working in a Spirited culture.

SPIRITED CULTURE REVIEW

The Spirited organization

- Values enthusiasm, optimism, and creativity.

- Exhibits a high-energy environment.

- Expects teamwork.

- Assumes participation in group activities outside work.

- Thrives on brainstorming.

- Offers a social and fun environment.

- Has frequent informal communication.

Downsides

- Lengthy and frequent meetings.

- Lack of follow-through to get new ideas implemented.

- May frequently change direction and focus.

- Logic and caution may be viewed unfavorably.

Direct style. If you have a Direct style and you are working in a Spirited environment, you may have these reactions. You may

- Enjoy the fast pace and the stream of ideas and new challenges.

- Appreciate that behaviors such as thinking on your feet are recognized and rewarded.

On the other hand, you may

- Get bogged down in meetings.

- Resent having to involve others in decisions that seem clear to you.

- Feel that the social aspects of the culture are a waste of time.

To make the best use of your Direct strengths without creating too much friction in a Spirited environment, be willing to spend some time listening to your colleagues' ideas. Offer your own, and show how you can help the organization achieve the results it desires. For example, if you were a Direct employee working at Talumbre, you could direct your attention toward the existing product, since that is clearly an area of need. Achieve some quick wins and immediate results, and you will improve the success of the company while gaining recognition for yourself.

Considerate style. If you are a Considerate and you are working in a Spirited culture, you are likely to experience any or all of these reactions. You may

- Appreciate the friendliness and social aspect of the environment.

- Like the positive energy and optimistic atmosphere.

- Enjoy participating in the group brainstorming sessions and other collaborative activities.

On the other hand, you may feel

- Overwhelmed by the constant need for change.

- Frustrated by the lack of stability and clear guidelines for accomplishing work.

- Anxious because of the constant pressure to be charismatic and influence others, since you prefer to wait and see what others think.

To create a smoother fit if you are a Considerate in a Spirited culture, focus on the team and collaborative tasks of your position. If you offer to handle the details of a project, not only will you be appreciated by those who don't want to handle details, but you will set yourself apart as someone who can follow through on projects and help move the organization forward. And that contribution to the group is something that will increase your job satisfaction. For example, at Talumbre, you could serve as a project manager, focusing on the nuts and bolts of the project, and thereby helping the founders get their new product to market faster.

Systematic style. If you are a Systematic working in a Spirited organization, you will struggle to fit in because you are opposite on both the assertiveness and the expressiveness dimensions. You may have any or all of the following reactions. You may

- Find the pervasive focus on brainstorming and innovation pointless, without a commitment to follow through.

- Feel that the optimistic atmosphere is superficial.

- Find that your independent work style is at odds with the Spirited environment.

On the other hand

- Your emphasis on logic and analysis are the very strengths that a Spirited organization needs if it is to be well rounded and successful.

For a Systematic in a Spirited culture, the key to gaining acceptance is to spend time with your colleagues, gain their trust and support, and then show them how your analytical and objective approach can add value to the overall functioning of the organization and increase its success. Using the Talumbre example, use your Systematic strength to research the information necessary to move the new product forward. If you discover negative or pessimistic information, consider presenting it as a series of alternatives so that others have something to choose from. In addition, prepare to discuss the emotional aspects of each alternative, even if you don't believe they should be factors in the decision making.

EXERCISE: ADAPT TO THE SPIRITED CULTURE

Now, apply your knowledge to your work situation. If your workplace exhibits a Spirited culture, then answer the following questions to help improve the relationships and results throughout your Spirited organization. Jot down your initial impressions and thoughts in a notebook (paper or electronic) for future reference.

* How could you help Directs not feel annoyed by all the socializing and talking?

* How could you help Considerates find stability and security?

* How could you help Systematics not feel frustrated by the scattered, chaotic atmosphere?

TRE BOUQUET: HOW'S YOUR FIT?

Tre Bouquet is a chain of floral shops featuring the finest and freshest flowers in unique arrangements. Its stated mission is to make each customer smile. Its business model emphasizes life balance for its employees. The majority of the florists and other employees in the local shops are part time but still receive benefits on a prorated scale.

At the corporate headquarters, many employees have the opportunity to telecommute, and some of them job-share. Daily interactions between colleagues and departments are friendly and pleasant. There is lots of information sharing among departments—too much, if you ask Dan, an employee in the finance department. When Dan is asked what he likes best about working at Tre Bouquet, he says he likes the relaxed atmosphere and the support and coopera- tion, which is noticeably more positive than at any other place he has worked. On the flip side, the emphasis on collaboration slows down decision making to the point where he fears that the company may miss out on opportunities that get mired in dis- cussions. In addition, he has noticed lots of "watercooler" talk (gossip), and sometimes he hears about petty resentments sim- mering between individuals or departments. But on the whole, Dan is happy and satisfied working at Tre Bouquet and has rec- ommended several acquaintances for positions at the company.

The executives at Tre Bouquet are facing a dilemma. They want to acquire another floral company, but they realize that they have a unique company culture, and they are concerned about whether or not the merger would be successful.

———

If you are a Considerate, you will probably enjoy working at Tre Bou- quet or in other Considerate style cultures (see the sidebar for a brief review of the Considerate culture). However, if you do not have a Con- siderate style, you may feel uncomfortable, frustrated, or even down- right unhappy working in this environment. Adapting your style can help you draw on your strengths while minimizing friction in a Considerate setting, whether you possess a Direct, Spirited, or Sys- tematic style.

Direct style. If you have a Direct style and you are working in a Con- siderate environment, you may feel out of place, since your style is the opposite of the Considerate style on both the assertiveness and the expressiveness dimensions. You may

- Find your colleagues to be too laid-back and emotional, while they may perceive you as brash and overly forceful.
- Want to make decisions and take actions that others would resist, or you may even be considered a "loose cannon" to be avoided.

On the other hand, you may

- Give the organization the confidence to make bold decisions and take risks.

CONSIDERATE CULTURE REVIEW

The Considerate organization

- Values harmony, loyalty, and cooperation.

- Has colleagues who are thoughtful, considerate, and humble.

- Operates using teamwork and collaboration.

- Offers a relaxed atmosphere.

- Promotes life balance for its employees.

- Offers a sociable environment.

- Feels like hanging out with friends.

Downsides

- Homogeneous thinking.

- A "devil's advocate" perspective may be unappreciated.

- Conflict is often swept under the rug, only to resurface later as gossip and resentment.

- Individual accomplishments may go unrecognized.

To make the most of your Direct style in a Considerate organization, invest time in cultivating relationships. Find opportunities for individual accomplishments while demonstrating cooperation. For example, in the case of Tre Bouquet, you could get involved in the proposed merger and help the executives see the benefits of the merger. However, you would need to make sure you present a balanced perspective and examine the drawbacks as well.

Spirited style. Someone with a Spirited style who is working in a Considerate environment may experience the following situations. You may

- Feel bored.

- Find the security and stability of a Considerate culture stifling.

- View your colleagues as uninspiring.

- Be viewed as unreliable or even a "flake."

On the other hand, you may

- Appreciate the friendly atmosphere and social aspects that the Considerate environment offers.

- Stand out in a Considerate culture by offering innovative ideas, as long as you take the time to gain buy-in from your colleagues.

For a more ideal fit with a Considerate culture, tone down the more flamboyant aspects of your style while maintaining your enthusiasm and optimism. If you show your colleagues that you are sincere, you will be able to influence others and help the organization face challenges and gain a competitive edge. For example, at Tre Bouquet, you or other Spirited individuals could look for opportunities to brainstorm new product lines or marketing ideas with colleagues at corporate headquarters, and perhaps even reach out to individual shops to develop relationships and support there.

Systematic style. If your style is Systematic, you can be fairly content working in a Considerate culture. You are likely to

- Get along with your coworkers.

- Feel comfortable with the pace of work and decision making.

- Feel appreciated by your colleagues for your thorough analysis and high-quality work.

On the other hand, you may

- Be put off by what you perceive as others being too intrusive into your personal life.

- Be viewed as cold and impersonal by your coworkers.

- Feel that your research and analysis are being ignored, as decisions are made that are not based on facts.

To improve your fit in a Considerate culture, open up and engage in more direct contact with your coworkers. Once you have established a relationship, your colleagues will be more likely to be receptive to your analytical, objective approach. For example, at Tre Bouquet, you could use your strengths to provide more fact-based information—such as analyzing the potential merger—to help the executives make better decisions. But you and other Systematic employees would need to invest some time in connecting with your colleagues first in order to gain their trust.

 ## EXERCISE: ADAPT TO THE CONSIDERATE CULTURE

Now, apply this information to your own situation. If your work environment reflects a Considerate style, then use the following questions to develop a plan to create a smoother working environment for all personality styles. Again, you may want to jot down your initial impressions and thoughts in a notebook (paper or electronic) for future reference.

- How could you help Directs handle the emotional sensitivity of the group?

- How could you help Spiriteds find excitement and high energy?

- How could you help Systematics not feel frustrated by the emotionally based decision making?

DOLARA: HOW'S YOUR FIT?

DOLARA is the Department of Licensing and Regulatory Affairs. DOLARA is responsible for the licensing of occupations and businesses. There are several major divisions, the largest of which is the Division of Registrations. Other divisions (as well as the administrative services to support these divisions) include the Divisions of Insurance, Banking, Real Estate, and Security; the Office of Consumer Rights; and the Office of Policy and Regulatory Reform. The stated mission of DOLARA (described in its 200-page strategic plan) is to protect the residents of the state from fraudulent individuals and businesses and to support and encourage a fair and competitive business environment. In addition to the other work it does, DOLARA tracks meeting notices and meeting minutes for 120 different boards under its jurisdiction.

One employee, Jason, says that the best thing about working for DOLARA is that his career path is clearly spelled out for him. He knows exactly what he needs to do to be promoted and receive raises. He appreciates the emphasis on quality and accuracy, and he feels that he is helping contribute to the well-being of the state's residents as he carries out his job. Jason describes working for DOLARA as predictable but not boring.

On the negative side, Jason knows that DOLARA has a reputation for being slow to adopt new technology, and he admits that some of the procedures for getting new systems approved seem overly bureaucratic and stifled by red tape.

Clearly, if you are comfortable working in a Systematic environment, then DOLARA is an excellent style fit for you (see the sidebar for a brief review of Systematic culture). However, if your style is not Systematic, then working for DOLARA may require some adjustments to your approach if you wish to succeed in the organization. Following are some tips that will help you survive and perhaps thrive if you are working for or plan to work for an organization with DOLARA's style profile. All three styles are covered: Direct, Spirited, and Considerate.

Direct style. If you are a Direct style individual, you may have one or more of these reactions to working in the DOLARA style environment. You may

- Feel frustrated at the slow pace of decision making.

- Want to light a fire under some of your colleagues to get them moving.

SYSTEMATIC CULTURE REVIEW

The Systematic organization

- Values high standards
- Focuses on providing exceptional quality
- Makes decisions logically through careful analysis
- Pays attention to details
- Expects accuracy
- Respects its employees' rights and privacy
- Has employees who are punctual and dependable
- Provides an environment that feels stable

Downsides

- Low sense of community or lack of camaraderie
- Little informal communication
- Low-energy environment
- Potential to miss opportunities because of risk avoidance

On the other hand, you may

- Relate to DOLARA's straightforward, unemotional style and emphasis on logic.

Even if your Direct style collides with a Systematic organization, you can use your style in a positive way. Use your Direct style to

- Quickly sum up the positive and negative consequences of a decision.
- Help others see that taking a risk can have a positive payoff.

While your Direct style might make you action oriented, that is, "It's better to ask for forgiveness than for permission," a Systematic organization is not likely to reward this type of enthusiasm. However, your Direct style many help you get ahead in the organization, since your natural inclination is toward engagement, control, and leading the way. For example, you might use your Direct style to gain access to the process for writing and updating the strategic plan at DOLARA, since seeing the big picture and focusing on goals and objectives is one of your strengths.

Spirited style. If you are a Spirited individual, you may have one or more of the following reactions to working in an environment like DOLARA. You may

- Feel like a fish out of water, since your style is diametrically opposite to the DOLARA culture.

- Become quickly bored with predictable tasks.

- Need to work harder to pay attention to the details and achieve the expected accuracy.

While your Spirited style might clash with the expectations of a Systematic organization, you can still use your style in a positive way. Use your Spirited style to

- Improve your organizational and thinking skills, that is, learn to present your ideas in a logical manner rather than in a random, stream-of-consciousness way.

- Become a valuable brainstorming asset (especially after you've improved the way you present your ideas).

- Add energy and optimism to the workplace.

- Stand out—in a positive way—in the organization.

In addition, your perceived uniqueness can help you succeed in other ways. You might use your Spirited style (and the attention the style draws to you) to get involved in meetings with consumer groups and business groups to discuss and brainstorm ideas for regulatory reform or other changes being implemented by DOLARA.

Considerate style. If your style is Considerate, you may have one or more of the following reactions to working in an environment like DOLARA. You may

- Feel disconnected, since a strong emphasis is placed on working independently.

- Long for a more collaborative atmosphere.

- Feel that the environment is cold and unfriendly, even if colleagues don't share your feelings.

While individuals with a Considerate style appreciate the stability and predictability of a Systematic environment and the slow and steady pace of work, they may not always see eye to eye with their colleagues or the organizational approach. Still, they can use their style to

- Build cohesiveness in the group (remembering to use a low-key approach).

- Show others that being trustworthy and trusting others can help the group work better together and accomplish more.

As a Considerate, you might consider correcting any mismatch in your current work environment by seeking out work in other parts of the organization that are better suited to your personality style. For example, you might search out work in DOLARA support services, including HR, or perhaps in the Office of Consumer Rights, where your style would be valued in the work of helping consumers resolve issues and get their needs met.

EXERCISE: ADAPT TO THE SYSTEMATIC CULTURE

At this point, you should have a good idea of how the three other personality styles fit into or clash with a Systematic organizational culture. Now it's time to apply any lessons learned to your own work situation. If you work in a Systematic culture, then work through the following questions to begin developing your own set of action items to better align your personality style with those of your team and your organization. Think carefully about the answers to these questions. Jot down your initial impressions and thoughts for future reference.

- How could you help Directs not feel frustrated by the slow pace of decision making?

- How could you help Spiriteds not get bored with the detail-oriented nature of the culture?

- How could you help Considerates not feel that they are being treated impersonally or feel disconnected from the rest of the group?

EXERCISE: BLOOM WHERE YOU'RE PLANTED

What is your personality style? _____

_____

_____

What is the style of your organization? _____

_____

_____

What factors in your work environment are pressuring you to adapt to the organization's style rather than using your natural style? _____

_____

_____

_____

What adjustments can you make to draw on your style strengths while avoiding stress or tension with others in your environment? _____

_____

_____

_____

▶ POINTS TO REMEMBER

- ▶ Characteristics of a Direct culture: values action and results; quick decision making; competitive; rewards individual accomplishments

  - If you have a Spirited style: selectively choose which ideas to promote; narrow your attention so that you don't appear scattered.

  - If you have a Considerate style: develop a thicker skin; reach out to a small group for support and encouragement.

  - If you have a Systematic style: pick one or two critical decisions and focus your detailed analysis on those; let other decisions be made with less thorough analysis.

- ▶ Characteristics of a Spirited culture: upbeat; optimistic; creative; social; lots of informal communication; focus and direction change frequently

  - If you have a Direct style: listen to others' ideas; use your drive to motivate the organization to take action.

  - If you have a Considerate style: focus on team and collaborative activities.

  - If you have a Systematic style: spend time with others to gain their trust and support, then show how objective analysis helps make better decisions.

- ▶ Characteristics of a Considerate culture: sociable; values teamwork and collaboration; slow decision making; avoids conflict

  - If you have a Direct style: invest time in cultivating relationships; find opportunities for individual accomplishments while demonstrating cooperation.

  - If you have a Spirited style: maintain your enthusiasm and optimism while slowing down your hyper pace.

- If you have a Systematic style: make a connection with others; understand that your objective analysis will be one aspect of decision making, but not the only one.

▶ Characteristics of a Systematic culture: high standards; slow decision making; lack of informal communication; respect for employees' rights and privacy

- If you have a Direct style: sum up the pros and cons of a decision to encourage risk taking; use your natural drive to encourage others to take action.

- If you have a Spirited style: present your ideas in a logical manner; show that they are well thought out and not half-baked.

- If you have a Considerate style: use a low-key approach to build a connection with others.

What's Your Personality Style?

At this point, you probably have a good idea of your personality style. The quick self-assessment that follows provides a tool to enable you to definitively identify your personality style. In addition to completing the assessment in the book, you can, for a small fee, take a comprehensive version of the assessment at www.personalitystyleat work.com. You will receive a style-specific, customized report that's full of tips and techniques that you can use to make the most of your style. Whichever method you choose to use to identify your personality style, I hope you will take advantage of the additional resources offered at www.personalitystyleatwork.com.

Self-Assessment

The self-assessment consists of 18 pairs of adjectives. For each pair, you will have a total of 5 points to divide between the two adjectives. Distribute the points based on how much each adjective describes you. Here's an example:

_____ Action-Oriented   _____ Animated

If you feel that *action-oriented* describes you completely and *animated* not at all, then you would assign 5 points to *action-oriented* and 0 points to *animated*. If you feel that *action-oriented* describes you somewhat, but *animated* describes you more, then you would assign 1 or 2 points to *action-oriented* and 3 or 4 points to *animated*. You can use any combination that adds up to 5 points, but do not use fractions. If you feel that both adjectives describe you equally, decide which adjective describes you just a bit more; you cannot divide the points equally.

Self-Assessment

1. a. _____ Action-Oriented   b. _____ Animated

2. a. _____ Detail-Oriented   b. _____ Sentimental

3. a. _____ Enthusiastic   b. _____ Appreciative

4. a. _____ Logical   b. _____ Dramatic

5. a. _____ Agreeable   b. _____ Diligent

6. a. _____ Precise   b. _____ Strong-Willed

7. a. _____ Candid   b. _____ Technical

8. a. _____ Adventurous   b. _____ Even-Tempered

9. a. _____ Thorough   b. _____ Stimulating

10. a. _____ Powerful   b. _____ Accurate

11. a. _____ Popular   b. _____ Impressive

12. a. _____ Consistent   b. _____ Cooperative

13. a. _____ Accommodating   b. _____ Challenging

14. a. _____ Patient   b. _____ Spontaneous

15. a. _____ Talkative   b. _____ Competitive

16. a. _____ Supportive   b. _____ Lively

17. a. _____ Optimistic   b. _____ Orderly

18. a. _____ Self-reliant   b. _____ Generous

Scoring

Transfer your numbers into the appropriate column. For example:

1. a. ___2___ Action-Oriented   b. ___3___ Animated

The number you assigned to 1. a. goes in the Direct column, and the number you assigned to 1. b. goes in the Spirited column. Continuing, the number you assigned to 2. a. goes in the Systematic column, and the number you assigned to 2. b. goes in the Considerate column.

After you have filled in your numbers in their respective columns, add up the numbers in each column. The totals for all four columns should add up to 90. The column with the highest total score is your dominant personality style.

Total Direct	Total Spirited	Total Considerate	Total Systematic
1. a. _____	1. b. _____	2. b. _____	2. a. _____
6. b. _____	3. a. _____	3. b. _____	4. a. _____
7. a. _____	4. b. _____	5. a. _____	5. b. _____
8. a. _____	9. b. _____	8. b. _____	6. a. _____
10. a. _____	11. a. _____	12. b. _____	7. b. _____
11. b. _____	14. b. _____	13. a. _____	9. a. _____
13. b. _____	15. a. _____	14. a. _____	10. b. _____
15. b. _____	16. b. _____	16. a. _____	12. a. _____
18. a. _____	17. a. _____	18. b. _____	17. b. _____
Total: _____	Total: _____	Total: _____	Total: _____

Your Dominant Personality Style: _____

About the HRDQ Style Model

Your personality sheds light on everything you do—the way you interact with others, perform as a team member, spend your free time, and lead employees. You name it. And before you can make meaningful improvements in your performance, you must first discover what makes you, well, undeniably *you*. As I mentioned at the beginning of the book, there are countless theories, models, and books about personality style. I wanted to share information that is simple yet useful. That's why I chose the HRDQ Style Model as the backbone of this book.

The result of years of expert research and development and proven theory, the HRDQ Style Model is the formula that thousands of individuals have relied upon not only to understand what makes them tick, but to understand those around them as well. The model takes the complexity of personality and boils it down into four simple, memorable words: *Direct, Spirited, Considerate,* and *Systematic.* The meaning behind these terms is the key to unlocking what drives human behavior. And as a seasoned author and training consultant—not to mention parent, friend, and spouse—I speak from experience when I say that I've tapped into this model more times than I can count.

For more than three decades, HRDQ has been a trusted developer of experiential learning resources that help to develop great people skills. Whether you are a frontline employee, a high-ranking executive, or just someone who is inspired to learn and grow as an individual, its resources are guaranteed to initiate lasting change and improvement. The HRDQ Style Model is no exception, and I'm excited that HRDQ has allowed me to share it with you.

So if you want to become better skilled at communicating with others, leading cross-functional teams, clinching lucrative deals, or building a healthy rapport with others, getting to know the HRDQ Style Model is the first step you should take. There isn't an easier, more powerful way to understand the impact your personality style has on your life, both personal and professional. You can learn more about HRDQ at www.hrdq.com.

NOTES

Chapter 1

1. Richard J. Gerrig and Philip G. Zimbardo, *Glossary of Psychological Terms*, http://www.apa.org/research/action/glossary.aspx.

Chapter 2

1. Robert E. Alberti and Michael L. Emmons, *Your Perfect Right: Assertiveness and Equality in Your Life and Relationships*, 9th ed. (Atascadero, CA: Impact Publishers, 2008).

Chapter 3

1. "Gallup's List of Most Widely Admired People of the 20th Century," Gallup Organization, December 1999; http://en.wikipedia.org/wiki/Gallup's_List_of_Most_Widely_Admired_People_of_the_20th_Century.
2. HRDQ, *What's My Learning Style?* (King of Prussia, PA: HRDQ, 2008).

Chapter 4

1. "Differences in Values," International Online Training Program on Intractable Conflict, Conflict Research Consortium, University of Colorado; http://www.colorado.edu/conflict/peace/problem/valdiff.htm, accessed November 20, 2011.
2. Jason Westland, *The Project Management Life Cycle: A Complete Step-by-Step Methodology for Initiating, Planning, Executing and Closing a Project Successfully* (London/Philadelphia: Kogan Page Ltd., 2007).
3. Ike Lasater with Julie Stiles. *Words That Work in Business: A Practical Guide to Effective Communication in the Workplace* (Encinitas, CA: PuddleDancer Press, 2010).
4. Kenneth Cloke and Joan Goldsmith, *Resolving Conflicts at Work: Ten Strategies for Everyone on the Job* (San Francisco: Jossey-Bass, 2011).

Chapter 5

1. Davis Foulger, "Models of the Communication Process," February 25, 2004; http://davis.foulger.info/research/unifiedModelOfCommunication.htm.

2. Jeanne Segal, Melinda Smith, and Jaelline Jaffe, "Nonverbal Communication: Improving Your Nonverbal Skills and Reading Body Language," Helpguide.org, November 2011; http://helpguide.org/mental/eq6_nonverbal_communication.htm#authors.
3. Michael H. Hoppe, *Active Listening: Improve Your Ability to Listen and Lead* (Greensboro, NC: Center for Creative Leadership, 2006).
4. Leon F. Seltzer, "Criticism vs. Feedback—Which One Wins, Hands-Down," *Evolution of the Self* (blog), June 30, 2009; http://www.psychologytoday.com/blog/evolution-the-self/200906/criticism-vs-feedback-which-one-wins-hands-down-part-1.

Chapter 6

1. Donald Clark, "The Art and Science of Leadership: A Complete Guide to Leadership," *Big Dog & Little Dog's Performance Juxtaposition*; http://www.nwlink.com/~donclark/leader/leader.html, accessed November 20, 2011.
2. Leigh Buchanan, "Managing One-to-One," *Inc.com*, October 1, 2001; http://www.inc.com/magazine/20011001/23479.html.
3. "Giving Effective Feedback," Holden Leadership Center, University of Oregon; http://leadership.uoregon.edu/resources/exercises_tips/skills/giving_effective_feedback, accessed November 20, 2011.
4. Chip Scholz, "What's Your Ratio of Positive to Negative at Work?" *Leader Snips, the Blog*, January 18, 2011, http://www.chipscholz.com/2011/01/18/whats-your-ratio-of-postive-to-negative-at-work/.
5. "Delegation: Delegating Authority, Skills, Tasks and the Process of Effective Delegation," *Businessballs.com*; http://www.businessballs.com/delegation.htm, accessed November 20, 2011.

Chapter 7

1. Patrick R. Laughlin, Erin C. Hatch, Jonathan S. Silver, and Lee Boh, "Groups Perform Better than the Best Individuals on Letters-to-Numbers Problems: Effect of Group Size," *Journal of Personality and Social Psychology*, 90, no. 4, April 2006; http://psychology.about.com/od/psychologynews/qt/groupsize.htm.
2. Eva Rykr, "Team Troubleshooting: Balancing Tasks and People," *The QuickBase Blog*, March 9, 2010; http://quickbase.intuit.com/blog/2010/03/09/team-troubleshooting-balancing-tasks-and-people/.
3. Judith Stein, "Decision-Making Models: Using Consensus Decision-Making to Increase Team Effectiveness," *Human Resources at MIT: Working on Teams*; http://web.mit.edu/hr/oed/learn/teams/art_decisions.html, accessed November 20, 2011.
4. Alyssa Gregory, "4 Elements of Trust Needed for Successful Collaboration," *Sitepoint.com*, July 7, 2010; http://www.sitepoint.com/4-elements-of-trust-for-collaboration/.
5. Stephen Wood, "What Is? Conflict in Teams," Institute of Work Psychology, University of Sheffield; http://esrccoi.group.shef.ac.uk/pdf/whatis/conflict.pdf, accessed November 20, 2011.

6. R. Meredith Belbin, *Team Roles at Work*, 2nd ed. (Oxford, UK: Butterworth Heinemann, 2010).

7. Kate Lister, "Workshifting Benefits: The Bottom Line," TeleworkResearchNet work.com, May 2010; http://www.workshifting.com/downloads/downloads/Workshifting%20Benefits-The%20Bottom%20Line.pdf.

8. "As More Employees Go 'Virtual', How Do We Keep Them Connected?," MSI: Knowledge Center, *Relocation Journal* (blog), April 29, 2011; http://www.relojournal.com/blogs/category/Technology.aspx.

Chapter 9

1. Charles Hughes, "Hughes' Views—Why Employees Stay," Center for Values Research; http://www.cvrdallas.com/hughes-view.html, accessed November 20, 2011.

2. Vanessa Fuhrmans, "VW-Suzuki Partnership Nears Collapse," *Wall Street Journal*, September 12, 2011.

3. Jeffrey Schmidt, *Making Mergers Work: The Strategic Importance of People* (Alexandria, VA: Society for Human Resource Management, 2004).

4. Carl Bialik, "Seven Careers in a Lifetime? Think Twice, Researchers Say," *Wall Street Journal*, September 4, 2010.

ACKNOWLEDGMENTS

Writing a book feels like a solitary endeavor when you're sitting in front of a computer for hours at a time and days on end. However, the reality is that publishing a book is a group effort. In my case, there are two people at the top of my list to thank for their help: Martin Delahoussaye and Mark Morrow. Simply put, without Martin, the VP of publishing at HRDQ, this book wouldn't have been written. Martin helped shape the vision of the book and was an invaluable resource in checking content accuracy as it related to the HRDQ Personality Style Model. As my development editor, Mark always delivered his edits with a healthy dose of encouragement. This book is stronger for his input. Thanks.

Martin, Mark, and I are a trio of Considerates, so as you would expect from this style, the process of working with them was positive and free from conflict. I highly recommend working with Considerates on any project requiring feedback, as it will be offered with genuine support and encouragement!

I also want to thank the team at McGraw-Hill for its attention to detail and its dedication to producing the highest-quality work.

And finally, I want to thank my family—my husband, Bill, and my sons, Eric and Ben. They left me alone when I needed to be left alone, and they gave me hugs when I needed a boost. And to my extended family and friends who willingly (or unwillingly) listened to me talk about "the book" at length—thanks for your patience and support.

Index

A

Accountability to team, 131–132
Action plan step (coaching model), 109
Active listening, 84–85
Aggression, assertiveness vs., 19
Analysis paralysis, 115
Analyze step (coaching model), 108
Assertiveness, 18–20
    aggression vs., 19
    comparing yourself to others in, 31–32
    in four personality styles, 27–28
    in language and behaviors, 20
    low-end behaviors of, 19

B

Behavior(s):
    assertive, 20
    leadership, 48–50
    of low and high expressiveness, 21
    passive, 19
    recognizing personality styles from, 45–47
Body language, as clue to personality style, 39–40
Boss, 149–173
    assessing work style of, 171–172
    getting along with, 150
    personality styles in working with, 13
    styles in boss-employee relationships, 151–171
Briggs, Katharine Cook, 7

C

Career choice (*see* Job–personality match)
Checking for understanding, 83
Choleric humor, 5, 6
Coaching, 107
    flexing style of, 110–111
    three-part coaching model, 108–109
Commitments, not following through on, 134
Communication, 79–97
    active listening, 84–85
    checking for understanding, 83
    in difficult situations, 92–96
    flexing messages for different styles, 88–92
    indirect, 82
    nonverbal, 39–40, 82–83
    personality style shortcomings, 86–88
    personality style strengths, 85–86
    preparation for, 80–82
    sending your message, 82–83
    three-step process for, 79–80
    virtual or remote, 51–53
Competence, 132
Concern, 133
Conflict, 57–76
    addressing, 65–66
    dealing with stress, 70–74
    escalation of, 69–70
    issues-based, 58, 66–68
    personality-based, 58, 65–66
    personality styles in, 11

Conflict (cont'd)
    resolving, 65–68
    and style compatibility, 58–63
    on teams, 135–138
    types of, 57–58
    values-based, 58
Confrontation model for addressing
    conflict, 65–66
Consensus, team, 129
Considerate quadrant (HRDQ), 8
Considerate style, 22, 28
    and active listening, 84
    body language with, 40
    in boss-employee relationships,
        153–156, 158–166, 169–170
    coaching by, 107, 110, 111
    communication shortcomings of,
        87–88
    communication strengths of, 85–86
    compatibility/conflict with other
        Considerates, 60–61
    compatibility/conflict with other
        styles, 59–61
    conflict handling by, 64
    in Considerate organization
        cultures, 213
    decision making by, 104
    and delegation, 116–119
    in Direct organization cultures, 206
    discussing sensitive situations with,
        94
    in escalating conflicts, 69, 70
    flexing your message for, 89–90
    giving constructive feedback to, 93
    handling mistakes with, 95
    in issues-based conflicts, 67, 68
    job-personality match for, 178, 185–
        187
    leadership by, 49, 101
    learning style of, 39
    motivating employees with, 105
    as organizational culture, 202, 203,
        212–216
    overdeveloped, 30
    preparation for communicating
        with, 80, 81
    problem solving by, 114
    and sending messages, 82, 83

Considerate style (cont'd)
    in Spirited organization cultures,
        210–211
    under stress, 72–73
    in Systematic organization cultures,
        220
    on teams, 46–47, 126, 127, 129–131,
        133, 135, 140–142, 146
    time management with, 45
    verbal communication by, 42–43
    virtual or remote communication
        by, 51
Constructive feedback, 92–93
Cooperation (on teams), 134–135
Criticism, as trust buster, 134
Culture, organizational (see
    Organizational culture/style)

D

Decision making:
    in envisioning the future, 103–104
    on teams, 129
Delegation, 115–121
    flexing style for, 118–120
    micromanaging, 120–121
    obstacles to, 117–118
    steps of, 115–116
Difficult situations, communication
    in, 92–96
Dimensions of personality, 17–32
    assertiveness, 18–20
    comparing yourself to others, 31–32
    expressiveness, 20–21
    overuse of, 29
    personality styles derived from, 21–29
Direct language, 82
Direct quadrant (HRDQ), 7, 8
Direct style, 22, 27
    and active listening, 84
    body language with, 40
    in boss-employee relationships,
        151–157, 161–162, 166–167
    coaching employees with, 109, 111
    communication shortcomings of,
        86–87
    communication strengths of, 85
    compatibility/conflict with other
        Directs, 60

Direct style (cont'd)
  compatibility/conflict with other
    styles, 58–60
  conflict handling by, 64
  in Considerate organization
    cultures, 213, 214
  decision making by, 104
  and delegation, 117, 118
  in Direct organization cultures, 204
  discussing sensitive situations with,
    94
  in escalating conflicts, 69, 70
  flexing your message for, 89–90
  giving constructive feedback to, 93
  handling mistakes with, 95
  in issues-based conflicts, 67, 68
  job–personality match for, 178, 182–
    183
  leadership by, 48, 100–102
  learning style of, 38–39
  motivating employees with, 105
  as organizational culture, 202–208
  overdeveloped, 29
  preparation for communicating
    with, 80, 81
  problem solving by, 114
  in Spirited organization cultures, 210
  under stress, 70–71
  in Systematic organization cultures,
    217–219
  on teams, 46, 126–131, 133, 140–142, 145
  time management with, 44
  verbal communication by, 42, 43
  virtual or remote communication
    by, 51

E
Einstein, Albert, 35
Elevator speech, 197
E-mails, recognizing personality
  styles in, 52–53
Emotions of Normal People, The
  (William Moulton Marston), 7
Encouraging others, 107–111
  flexing your coaching style for, 110–
    111
  three-part coaching model for, 108–
    109

Engaging others, 104–107
Envisioning the future, 101–104
  decision making, 103–104
  weighing options, 102–103
Escalation of conflict, 69–70
Executing results, 112–115
Expressiveness, 20–21
  comparing yourself to others, 31–32
  in four personality styles, 27–28

F
Feedback, giving, 92–93
Feedback step (coaching model), 108–
  109
Friedman, Howard S., 5

G
Gates, Bill, 99
"Go slow" approach, 114
Ground rules (teams), 128–129
Groupthink, avoiding, 130

H
Hippocrates, 5
HRDQ Personality Style Model, xiv,
  7–9, 227–228
Hughes, Charles, 189
Humors, 5–6

I
Indirect communication, 82
Informing, as purpose of
  communication, 80
Inquiry, as purpose of
  communication, 80
Intent, 132–133
Issues-based conflict, 58, 66–68

J
Job search strategies, 196–199
Job–personality match, 177–200
  for Considerate style, 185–187
  culture quiz for, 179–180
  for Direct style, 182–183
  job search strategies for, 196–199
  organizational culture in, 191–196
  skills inventory for, 180–181
  for Spirited style, 184–185

Job–personality match (*cont'd*)
for Systematic style, 187–189
work setting in, 189–191
Jobs, Steve, 102
Jung, Carl, 6, 7

K

King, Martin Luther, Jr., 35

L

Language, assertive, 20
Leadership, 99–123
delegation in, 115–121
encouraging others in, 107–111
engaging others in, 104–107
envisioning the future in, 101–104
executing results in, 112–115
qualities of a great leader, 100
styles of, 100
Leadership behavior and recognizing
personality styles, 48–50
Leadership styles, 100
Learning style as clue to personality
style, 38–39
Listening:
active, 84–85
recognizing personality styles by,
41–43
Lying as trust buster, 134

M

Mandela, Nelson, 99, 100
Marston, William Moulton, 6, 7
MBTI (Myers-Briggs Type Indicator), 7
Melancholic humor, 5, 6
Micromanaging, 120–121
Motivating employees, 105–107
Myers, Isabel Briggs, 7
Myers-Briggs Type Indicator (MBTI), 7

N

Networking, 198
Nonverbal communication, 39–40,
82–83
Norms (teams), 128–129

O

Observation, recognizing personality
styles by, 36–40

Occupation, choice of (*see* Job-
personality match)
Organizational culture/style, 179–180,
201–223
Considerate, 202, 203, 212–216
Direct, 202–208
and personality style, 191–196
Spirited, 202, 203, 208–212
Systematic, 202, 203, 216–221

P

Passive behavior, 19
Performance goals, for teams, 128
Performance standards, 112–113
Personality:
defined, 4
understanding of, 5–7
Personality (Howard S. Friedman and
Miriam W. Schustack), 5
Personality style(s), xiii–xiv, 3–15
defined, 5
importance of understanding, 9–14
overuse of, 29–31
self-assessment of, 225–227
(*See also each style, e.g.: Direct style*)
Personality-based conflict, 58, 65–66
Persuasion:
personality styles in, 11–12
as purpose of communication, 80
Phlegmatic humor, 5, 6
Pierret, Chuck, 196
Preparation for communication, 80–82
Problem solving, 114

R

Recognizing personality styles, 35–55
exercise for, 43–44
from leadership behavior, 48–50
by listening, 41–43
by observing, 36–40
from team behavior, 45–47
from time management, 44–45
in virtual or remote worlds, 50–53
Relationship issues for teams, 132–138
Relationship-based conflict, 136–138
Reliability, 132–133
Remote interactions, recognizing
personality styles in, 50–53
Results, executing, 112–115

S

Sanguine humor, 5, 6
Schustack, Miriam W., 5
Sending your message, 82–83
Skills inventory, 180–181
Spirited quadrant (HRDQ), 7, 8
Spirited style, 22, 27–28
  body language with, 40
  in boss-employee relationships,
    152–153, 156–163, 167–169
  coaching employees with, 109–111
  communication shortcomings of, 87
  communication strengths of, 85
  compatibility/conflict with other
    Spiriteds, 60
  compatibility/conflict with other
    styles, 58–60
  conflict handling by, 64
  in Considerate organization
    cultures, 214–215
  decision making by, 104
  and delegation, 117–119
  in Direct organization cultures,
    204–206
  discussing sensitive situations with,
    94
  in escalating conflicts, 69
  flexing your message for, 89, 90
  giving constructive feedback to, 93
  handling mistakes with, 95
  in issues-based conflicts, 67–68
  job–personality match for, 178, 184–185
  leadership by, 48–49, 101
  learning style of, 39
  motivating employees with, 105
  as organizational culture, 202, 203,
    208–212
  overdeveloped, 29–30
  preparation for communicating
    with, 80, 81
  problem solving by, 114
  and sending messages, 82
  in Spirited organization cultures, 209
  under stress, 71–72
  in Systematic organization cultures,
    219
  on teams, 46, 126, 127, 129, 130, 133,
    135, 140–142, 145–146

Spirited style (cont'd)
  time management with, 44–45
  verbal communication by, 42, 43
  virtual or remote communication
    by, 51
Stereotyping, danger of, 10
Stress, dealing with styles under, 70–74
Style, organizational (see
    Organizational culture/style)
Style-based conflict (see Personality-
    based conflict)
Support (on teams), 135
Systematic quadrant (HRDQ), 8
Systematic style, 22, 28–29
  body language with, 40
  in boss-employee relationships,
    155–156, 160–161, 165–171
  coaching employees with, 110, 111
  communication shortcomings of, 88
  communication strengths of, 86
  compatibility/conflict with other
    styles, 59, 60
  compatibility/conflict with other
    Systematics, 60–61
  conflict handling by, 65
  in Considerate organization
    cultures, 215–216
  decision making by, 104
  and delegation, 117–119
  in Direct organization cultures,
    206–207
  discussing sensitive situations with,
    94
  in escalating conflicts, 69
  flexing your message for, 89, 91
  giving constructive feedback to, 93
  handling mistakes with, 95
  in issues-based conflicts, 67, 68
  job–personality match for, 178, 187–189
  leadership by, 49, 101
  learning style of, 39
  motivating employees with, 106
  as organizational culture, 202, 203,
    216–221
  overdeveloped, 30–31
  preparation for communicating
    with, 80, 81
  problem solving by, 114, 115

Systematic style (*cont'd*)
   and sending messages, 82, 83
   in Spirited organization cultures,
      211–212
   under stress, 73–74
   in Systematic organization cultures,
      217
   on teams, 47, 126, 127, 129, 130, 133,
      140–142, 146
   time management with, 45
   verbal communication by, 43
   virtual or remote communication
      by, 51–52

T

Task-based conflict, 136–138
Team behavior, recognizing
   personality styles from, 45–47
Teams, 125–148
   personality styles on, 12–13
   positive and productive, 127–128
   relationship issues for, 132–138
   roles on, 138–144
   style strengths in, 126–127
   tasks of, 128–132
   virtual, 144–146
Temperaments, 5–6
Teresa, Mother, 35
Thatcher, Margaret, 35
Three-part coaching model, 108–109
Three-step communication process,
   79–83
   checking for understanding, 83
   preparing yourself and the other
      person for, 80–82
   sending your message, 82–83

Time, trust and, 133
Time management, recognizing
   personality styles from, 44–45
Trump, Donald, 99
Trust, 132–134

U

Understanding, checking for, 83

V

Values-based conflicts, 58
Verbal communication, personality
   style and, 42–43
Virtual interactions, recognizing
   personality styles in, 50–53
Virtual teams, 144–146
Vision, 101 (*See also* Envisioning the
   future)

W

Winfrey, Oprah, 99
Winterkorn, Martin, 189
Work approach/methods, for teams,
   128–129
Work setting, 189–191
Workplace choice, personality styles
   in, 13–14
Workspace, as clue to personality
   style, 36–38

Y

Yellow bile, 5, 6

ABOUT THE AUTHOR

With more than 20 years of experience, Kate Ward has an impressive track record in training development. She began her career as a manager of curriculum development for CareerTrack, where she authored programs, supervised a team of instructional designers, and facilitated training. She also served as the senior instructional designer at TreeLine Training, responsible for leading the development of the core skills curriculum library. Kate is currently running her own company, working to create innovative training solutions for today's business needs.

About **HRDQ**

For more than 30 years, HRDQ has been a trusted developer and publisher of experiential learning resources that help to improve the performance of individuals, teams, and organizations. It offers a wide range of research-based training materials including assessments, games, customizable programs, and e-learning workshops on today's most in-demand soft-skills topics such as leadership, communication, coaching, and team building.

At the core of every product is the HRDQ Experiential Learning Model™, a powerful formula that combines a mixture of organizational theory and proven facilitation methods with a high level of interaction and an appreciation for adult learning styles to make learning stick. From frontline employees to senior-level executives and everyone in between, HRDQ's training solutions are guaranteed to initiate lasting change and generate a return on investment.

HRDQ's primary audience includes Fortune 500 companies, corporate trainers, human resource professionals, educational institutions, and organizational development consultants. Its flagship product line, the HRDQ Style Series™, has been used by millions of people around the world to achieve measurable performance improvements. This comprehensive family of assessments, games, books, and activities provides individuals, teams, and even entire organizations with an effective means for understanding and internalizing how personality drives behavior, impacts relationships, and influences leaders. Perennial favorites, such as the bestselling *Jungle Escape* game, the award-winning *Mars Surface Rover*, and the customizable *Reproducible Training Library* make HRDQ a go-to resource for novice trainers and seasoned facilitators alike.